Edward Novoa graduated with a master of arts degree from Pratt Institute, NY, in 1992. He has been a life-long entrepreneur and international designer.

After traveling 25 countries and living in three, he was intrigued by the singularity of American culture. Ethics, philosophy, religion, and capitalism are some of the topics that are discussed in a fluid narrative illustrated with film analysis, storytelling, and a thorough research on scholars and writers. Shocked as an immigrant, he decided to write his insight on very tangible contradictions.

He has raised his voice against populism in Latin America, especially in Mexico, where a socialist dictatorship is trying to take over the Mexican democracy. With a clear and philosophical discourse, he has contributed to uncover to the public the dark inspirations of the government. He has been interviewed by several news programs and his political analyses have been broadcasted in different media outlets.

To my three children, Natalia, Camila, and Sebastian.
To my father, pediatrician and writer.
To Dennise.
To the American people for whom I feel admiration and
am concerned about.

Edward Novoa

The American

A Compelling Analysis of Our Contradictions

Austin Macauley Publishers™

London • Cambridge • New York • Sharjah

Ordering Information
Quantity sales: Special discounts are available on quantity purchases by corporations, associations, and others. For details, contact the publisher at the address below.

Publisher's Cataloging-in-Publication data
Novoa, Edward
The American

ISBN 9798886937336 (Paperback)
ISBN 9798886937343 (ePub e-book)

Library of Congress Control Number: 2023920671

www.austinmacauley.com/us

First Published 2024
Austin Macauley Publishers LLC
40 Wall Street, 33rd Floor, Suite 3302
New York, NY 10005
USA

mail-usa@austinmacauley.com
+1 (646) 5125767

With thanks to:

Jose Novoa, psychiatrist
Javier Novoa, psychologist

Table of Contents

Foreword

The mistake is the motor of history.
Ikram Antaki

This book analyzes several contradictions that are deeply rooted in the culture as seen from outside, that is, from a newly arrived immigrant. These contradictions are also seen as an insider because I have lived in this country intermittently during my childhood, adolescence, young adulthood, and today. Needless to say, except for American Indians, all other Americans are immigrants or descendants of immigrants. This book will make the reader face some of the causes of anger of the American society. I also suggest some antidotes to these contradictions.

The questions I raise may move us away from our comfort zone. This book will give insight to problems that are rarely outspoken or if spoken of, minimized. It analyzes some of the symptoms of the underlying morality crisis.

My intention is fair; I hope that this book will transform us into better persons, including myself. I expect to sow awareness of the need of better actions and better attitudes.

"Not just individuals but whole nations, cultures, and societies need to be able to view themselves from the outside so as to have a crack of becoming as healthy as possible…the Observing Self is the ability to observe and react to our own behaviors as if they were the actions of someone else. *(Mark Terrel. "The Observing Self" unk.com/blog)"*

Introduction

We perceive life differently according to our age. I spent several summers as an exchange student living in Tacoma, surrounded by nature, with my American family. As children, our summer activities were playing games, doing our chores, enjoying Puget Sound, and going to church. I had a happy childhood and a nurturing experience in America.

When I studied my master's degree in Brooklyn, NY, my life was about studying, being creative, and investigating the Design world. Going to museums, design exhibits, tradeshows, theater, and concerts were my extracurricular activities.

Now that I came back to the US to work, life is about making money through providing a good service and product, following the law, and dealing with a vindictive and somewhat angry society.

American Character Traits

In spite of cultural differences and past military interventions, Americans have earned our respect along the years for many reasons. We acknowledge that America has a strong economy and a powerful army with historical successes, such as having defeated Hitler. We know that it is a leading technological force with high quality standards. It has many of the best universities and hospitals in the world. We admire its remarkable democracy and organized society. Many people believe that Americans are friendly because they are always eager to say 'Hi' and are polite. They are believed to be wealthy.

True or false, and not coincidentally but intentionally, this has also been the rhetoric of the film and media industries. For a person living in a foreign country, it is hard to understand the difference between the fiction created by these industries and reality. An immigrant comes to understand it later on.

In the local news, I listen that America is the best country in the world to live in, a superpower, a free country, and the place where immigrants fulfill their dreams. It is implied that nearly anybody in the world would love to become an American. I wonder if this is a dose of daily broadcasted *soma* or if there is truth in it. Either way, it is a national belief. (Soma is a type of recreational drug. It could be used to cure any sort of unhappiness within society. Brave New World, Aldous Huxley. 1932.)

Becoming an immigrant, however, confronts us with a different reality. First generation immigrants coincide in their appreciations of cultural differences with Americans. There is a charming politeness and a lack of courtesy. Politeness is rich in greetings and trivial conversations. Americans are very formal in their communications and express their gratitude. They will thank your attention and time, your punctuality and hard work. Their lack of courtesy will show in rough manners and selfish behavior. Americans practice social distancing not only as a result of a pandemic, but as a defensive attitude toward the other and are difficult to make friends with.

The greeting, as in many other cultures, is a defying nonverbal communication with chest up front and a look in the eye, as opposed to the oriental greeting that bows and does not make eye contact. A friendly 'hi' many times is a shield against confrontation. Citizens feel that they are being trespassed in their territory, social or personal proximity, job, spouse, children, friends, pets, vehicles, sidewalk space, crossing pedestrian space; anything that can be claimed as permanently or temporarily owned and cannot be claimed by the other. However, the boundaries may not be so obvious if we analyze abstract concepts such as liberty, or whose sidewalk space belongs to whom.

It is a country where banks and government support entrepreneurism, generating thousands of success stories and wealth. The common worker is paid low salaries.

Many Americans do not care much about their clothes, contradictorily with the presence of brands and marketing, perhaps because in the past, Puritanism dictated austere clothing. They like to dress comfortably. Clothes not often reflect income or taste and there is little formality when assisting to social gatherings, which most of the times are informal. While big amounts of money are spent on vehicles, properties, and appliances, not much money is spent on formal clothes.

It is a society in constant change that creates new words and phrases, which soon become part of a national new vocabulary. New words are challenging and enhance intelligence.

Americans are hardworking people that dedicate little time to have fun. 'To have fun' in America has a different meaning than 'to have fun' in other countries. For many of us, it means having reasons to laugh, preferably out loud, in company of friends and family, with or without alcohol.

For Americans, to have fun can mean all this, but also to practice a sport seriously, to spend time fixing or installing something following instructions, to work after hours, watch TV, or read. The main difference is that laughter is not necessarily involved while for other cultures, if there is no laughter, there is hardly any fun at all.

Americans have a peculiar sense of humor. I saw the movie 'I am Cuba' (Mikhail Kalatozov, 1964) in a movie theater in The Village, New York. It is a work of art; it was filmed in the 60s, in black and white. Its purpose was to romanticize and idealize the Cuban revolution. The movie is tragic, patriotic, epic, and idealistic. It is a dramatized documentary and in no way is it a comedy. There is not a single scene that can be funny, from my perspective. People would burst out in laughter throughout the movie, being a scene with an outraged prostitute one of them.

America is formed by immigrant groups as we know. The founders came from northern Europe, and so are its law, culture, and religion.

Indian extermination by the newly arrived Europeans to the colonies is something that is not frequently acknowledged. It must have been a barbarian and extensive bloodshed but it simply got buried in the past, as in any other colonization that happened throughout the world. On the contrary, bringing slaves from Africa that later on gained their freedom with much struggles, sets a turbulent but eventually in process of being normalized coexistence.

New immigrants need to merge into the mainstream of Anglo culture and they do so by speaking English in the first place, secondly by following laws and rules, and thirdly by exerting dominance. Because dominance and leadership are praised and fostered, individuals relish with their gains. To follow rules is not enough; the true citizen has to be an advocate of rules. Once an immigrant does these three things, he is in the process of being Americanized.

Americans like to act as a group and enjoy belonging to the group. This is one of the greatest assets of this country. They like to have similar activities, watch broadcasted sports, and use the same brands. They know how to work as a team toward common goals, both in small groups, as well as a whole country. In a way, individualism and collectivism coexist harmonically. They are open to be dictated opinions, which are administered by media and shared by the people. Americans enjoy doing what their co-nationals do and follow the trends, unlike other countries where individuals want to be different from their neighbors.

There is a high level of communitarian participation that has historically improved society. People care for each other. The main tool for this organization is establishing rules, that later on become laws. Laws are the foundation of social life. Americans are law abiding citizens and have brought the country to become a world leader as a republic and a democracy. It is a common belief that the country has the right to be the policeman of the world.

Exceptionalism, as explained by Jeffrey Sachs, is the belief that America is an exceptional country that has the right to punish, set global rules, impose military actions, and dictate economic measures as a result of being well positioned at the end of World War II, and of deeply rooted cultural traits. This belief is not correct for many reasons and harms the country… (Rob Johnson interview with Jeffrey Sachs about his book, A New Foreign Policy: Beyond American Exceptionalism, Columbia University Press, 2018)

Auto criticism is well taken by Americans but their pride and nationalism are stronger. Americans are proud of their nationality and some truly believe that their country is the greatest country in the world. However, every culture and country is a world in itself, and citizens of other countries think the same about their own country.

Many Americans are ready to claim that they are being trespassed and are prone to threaten; they aggressively claim their right to be paid. To do the right thing is preponderant. Many will feel guilty and apologize immediately. The consciousness of the other is overwhelming; the average 'good' citizen will only act if the other is not trespassed, at least superficially. A good citizen will say 'I am sorry' to strangers many times a day out of consideration and in order to avoid conflicts. There is a school teacher in every person; there is an introjected policeman in every citizen. Innocent Americans are constantly punished by their fellow citizens and by law enforcement officials in a preventive fashion for unimportant mistakes. This practice is carried out to impede people from becoming depraved.

Americans are isolated, every home is an island. Parents enjoy children but can't wait when the immature young adults will leave home to go to college and for good, only to meet again in Thanksgiving and a few other holidays; parents will be resentful for that. The country is vast; family and close friends get separated along life and across all the states. In other countries, children live in their homes throughout college until they are economically independent or get married.

Handshaking and some hugging are common. The lack of a greater physical contact creates a void, a longing. Social media is full of videos of animals and pets caressing each other, yet in America and other countries that are under an abundant legislation, touching is an alert of sexual harassment. Touching is unwanted closeness, relationships are a risk, and solitude is safe. As affection is avoided, individuals are resentful for feeling alone and separated. They are also resentful for the separateness created by generalized mistrust.

It has been said for decades that Americans have no culture. The seven fine arts have not flourished as they have in other colonized countries. The past is gone. There will never be a Classic period or a Renaissance because they happened before the country existed as such, and not much can be done about it. Still, arts and culture are flourishing little in the technological American world. Americans are good readers.

"Americans are ignorant and Europeans are cult" is a cliché. There is so much knowledge to be taught that it can only be classified and prioritized. Perhaps Puritanism gave little room to life enjoyment and contemplation through art (art is produced in leisure time, Protestantism promoted work and no leisure) while the idea of being a civilization chosen by God 'the city upon a hill' gave little room for a need of universality.

> "We shall be as a city upon a hill; the eyes of all people are upon us…a model of Christian Charity" (Governor John Winthrop, 1630) The passengers of the *Arbella* who left England in 1630 with their new charter had a great vision. They were to be an example for the rest of the world in rightful living. *(https://www.ushistory.org/us/3c.asp)*

Schools keep students poorly prepared in subjects such as Geography, Universal Literature, Universal History, and Philosophy, making young citizens believe that the rest of the world serves the purpose of being or not being of use to the country.

English is taught extensively and people have excellent skills in communicating and reading, making it easy for work to flow and generate results. Ethical behavior in schools is well taught and enforced, creating a reliable society. Sports are magnificently fostered creating a culture of excellence and achievement.

Needless to mention, a booming economy seems to be the center of society. America is undoubtedly a great country, with contradictions of similar size.

Contradiction 1
Are Law and Law Enforcement Creating a Happier Society?

Law procures a harmonic social environment where individuals respect each other, enhancing peace and happiness. Contradictorily, ruling all does limit all and neglects happiness.

"Good and evil: it is a dream to separate them and utopia to reconcile them." (Michel Onfray)

Civilizations have created law to achieve order and well-being. In theory, it is by consensus that human beings will abide by the rules they create to live respectfully to each other. This principle would lead us to believe that the more quantity of laws, the merrier the society will be. The outcome is rather opposite.

Some facts about law and law enforcement:

What is the country with more laws?

The US.

How many laws are there in the US?

"It is impossible for anyone to know all of the laws that affect them and it is, therefore, impossible to not break any laws. How many of the **4,450** crimes have you broken?" (John McAfee on February 7, 2013, whoismacafee.com)

"The most recent attempt at an official estimate from the Justice Department, completed more than 35 years ago, found…more than 3,000 crimes in statute, a number that may well have doubled since then…With so many different laws on the books…prosecutors can threaten decades in prison for acts that may amount to simple bad judgment. This is the opposite of the system of limited and clear laws that the framers of the Constitution had intended…Criminal laws threaten prison sentences for offenses ranging from trafficking in snakehead fish to selling mattresses without warning tags. Moreover, states and localities maintain so many criminal laws on the book that nobody even ventures a comprehensive count." *(Eli Lehrer, December 2, 2019, www.thehill.com)*

Harvard University professor Harvey Silverglate estimates that daily life in the United States is so over-criminalized, the average American professional commits about three felonies a day. (10 jun. 2015, Institute for Policy Studies, ips-dc.org)

What rank is America in freedom? 15th

(https://worldpopulationreview.com/country-rankings/freest-countries)

What rank is America in freedom? 53rd (The Freedom in the World 2020 report, produced by Freedom House) ranks the United States 53rd among 84 countries described as 'free' (as opposed to 'partly free' or 'not free'), sandwiched between Slovakia and Belize.

What is the country with more inmates? US

How many inmates are in America? 2.3 million.

What are the countries with more law enforcement (number of police officers)?

China, India, and the US.

Law enforcement describes the agencies and employees responsible for enforcing laws, maintaining public order, and managing public safety. The primary duties of law enforcement include the investigation, apprehension, and detention of individuals suspected of criminal offenses. (Google answer to: What is Law Enforcement? June 6, 2021)

There are more than 800,000 sworn law enforcement officers now serving in the United States, which is the highest figure ever. About 12 percent of those are female. There have been **56,034** assaults against law enforcement officers in 2019 (153 per day)

Established in 1845, The New York City Police Department (NYPD) is one of the most well-known law enforcement agencies in the world. As the largest in the US, it currently has about 36,008 full-time active officers and 19,000 civilian employees.

Today, the U.S. collectively spends **$100 billion** a year on policing and a further **$80 billion** on incarceration.

It's **often** reported that nearly 1 in 3 American adults, or about 30%, has a police record.

Having read the above information, some conclusions can be drawn. Seen in context with other countries, America is not as free of a country as it seems; the freedom that citizens enjoy ranks not number one, but number 15 according to one source, 53 according to another. However, it is believed to be the leader of the free world. America has as many inmates as Parisians live in Paris. America is the country with more laws and inmates (25% of world's incarcerations).

Laws were created because of the coexistence of good and evil in the human being according to Baudrillard, or by the vicious character of humans, according to Epictetus (Enquiridion). Good and evil would then be a cause of behavior and actions inherent in human nature and either one cannot exist without the other.

> "Good and evil coexist ever since the origin (symbolically) in the Garden of Eden. To ignore the evil in presence of the good and vice versa is absurd. Evil cannot be eliminated from human beings because we are contradictory beings as well. In the modern world, trying to differentiate good from evil, beauty from ugliness, and truth from falsehood has become senseless." (Jean Baudrillard La Trasparence du Mal)

When the French Revolution took place in 1789, monarchies started their transformation into republics. Jean Jacques Rousseau (1712–1778), explains in 'The Social Contract' (1762) that citizens are all equal to the law, empowered by the Social Contract to live in a new society where the figure of the King exists no more, and a republic is created. Voting is only the prelude to democracy and it is extended to a vast participation and representation of individuals in policies.

There are two principles of law that have to do with law enforcement:

1. Law is backed up by coercive authority.
2. In order to combat violent crime, the law has the monopoly of violence.

There is no question about the need and efficacy of law and law enforcement in making order prevail. American social functionality is based on them.

Ideally, when laws are written by general consensus, the ethical individual will follow them by reasoning. When reasoning fails and laws are broken, law enforcement appears. Law enforcement would then be a result of two things:

1. The failure of the system, as some individuals fail to learn to reason their desires
2. The unavoidable coexistence of good and evil

In a republic, the liberty of a man ends where the freedom of the other begins. In theory, a happy individual in society will not need to transgress because he will be free of resentment and guided by morality (Philosophy and Happiness, radio interview, Ikram Antaki).

Sergio Perez, professor of philosophy, explains German philosopher G.W. Hegel (1770–1831):

> "Because wherever there is a 'must be', there is an attack on freedom. By absolutizing duty, it has fragmented man and does not cease to suggest that he oppresses his natural impulses. Raising the commandments of morality to the rank of principles of reason, means acting against inclinations out of respect for duty, establishing 'a permanent contradiction between the heart and the head'."

Man will be in constant conflict between his own passions and reason. It is through reason that he will turn his passions into virtues. According to Hegel, the virtuous individual will comply with law out of understanding.

> "Hegel strives to offer a different vision: he affirms that the freedom that is available to the individual does not consist in suppressing his passions but in modifying the relationship he has with them… Desires and inclinations form one with the individual. That is why the individual must model them… 'we call it virtue when the passions are so related to reason that they do what reason orders'."

Hegel explains that freedom is a social condition gained after centuries of oppression and slavery. Sergio Perez continues, "Freedom is not a simple idea that emerged from the human imagination and it does not belong to the code of innate ideas of man. It is a category that results from the experience of universal history, which human beings know and have reached through the progressive rejection of various forms of oppression…Today, freedom has become a natural and inalienable right, but its nature is historical, the result of a long and tumultuous human process… Freedom is therefore a concept (it is) knowledge and not only an ideal. For that reason, freedom has an effective foundation and not just an imaginary foundation." (Perez, Sergio. Hegel: his concept of freedom)

Socially speaking, freedom then is not a dream or a yearning; it is the opposite to all forms of oppression, i.e. slavery, classicism, racism, male chauvinism, dictatorships, as well as religious and political persecutions.

An excess of ethicality could also become a form of oppression, therefore the importance of not exceeding ruling beyond rational understanding of citizens, and beyond allowing a reasonable flow of human activities in everyday life. Since the citizen cannot question or oppose the law because he will be taken as a felon, oppression will find escape valves that will manifest in inadequate adult behavior which is the inspiration of this book.

Permissiveness Versus Unforgiveness

When a society is permissive (through fewer laws and low law enforcement), individuals are permissive. When a society is unforgiving (through more laws and high law enforcement), individuals are unforgiving.

In permissiveness, and when the individuals are poorly educated, crime and trespasses take place. In order to (according to Hegel) align passion, desires, and reason, a better ethical education will be the solution, provided there are enough economic opportunities.

In permissiveness, human relationships are enjoyed and nurtured, people are allowed to touch and hug, to greet people with one or more kisses is common, and humane behavior prevails over compliance. Fallibility is normal as people are allowed to make mistakes, to be late, or lie (within limits) without being held accountable.

In unforgiveness, human relationships break and the happiness obtained through social contact is framed by correctness. Human fallibility becomes a punishable imperfection. To be late is reprehensible, to lie is unacceptable. Unforgiveness leads to perfectionism and solitude.

"The United States is a country that is the envy of the world for many reasons. One of the main reasons people from all over the world flock to our shores is because we live under the rule of law. We have a written Constitution and a Bill of Rights that

This particular point of view may have some truth in it. What should be analyzed further is the contradiction of being safe versus the fear of becoming a felon. In unforgiveness, the other will be punished for his trespasses against the individual, and this will make the individual feel safe. However, it is a two-way street and the trespasses of the individual against the other will also be punished. All are prone to be punished.

New technologies, companies, and activities will require more and new legislations. Can we imagine a ceiling to the number of laws, and if so, how many more will each individual break per day?

"Every solution creates a new problem." (Ikram Antaki, Toward a Citizen Ethics, You Tube, 2000)

The amount of laws and law enforcement is directly proportional to unforgiveness/intolerance and inversely proportional to permissiveness/ tolerance.

When a society enforces law vertically and relentlessly, people are afraid to be free even within their own boundaries; with an excess of rules, boundaries become confusing.

Perhaps not one country today has achieved social harmony, individual happiness, and prosperity altogether. European and Asian countries also have abundant laws. Different studies and statistics favor one country or another measuring economics, social equality, and happiness.

Unforgiveness is not an isolated consequence of highly restrictive societies. In fact, it is because they are unforgiving that so many laws are written. In the XVII and XVIII centuries, when America was founded, religion was the center of social life. If we want to find the causes of unforgiveness, we necessarily have to analyze two things:

1. History
2. Religion

In chapters 6 and 7, related topics of American religion are explained.

There would seem to be a middle point to be searched between unforgiveness and permissiveness, intolerance and tolerance that would enhance law and order, and at the same time allow for proximity, trust, and forgiveness among individuals.

Lawyers and Litigation

Law has become a powerful business that keeps the judiciary system and lawyers running. Many jobs and families depend on it. Capitalism promotes all consumer goods and services, including law services. Good and evil are also a business. The question is not what thousands of laws and law enforcement do to society. The question is what they do not do.

"The Most Litigious Countries in the World:

With a growing number of lawyers every year, lawyer totals are on the upswing in numerous countries. According to the American Bar Association, there are currently 1,116,967 lawyers practicing in the United States, which relates to about one for every 300 people. Here's a list of countries with the highest number of lawyers per capita:

1. U.S. 1 lawyer for every 300 people
2. Brazil: 1 lawyer for every 326 people
3. New Zealand: 1 lawyer for every 391 people
4. Spain: 1 lawyer for every 395 people
5. UK: 1 lawyer for every 401 people"
6. *(www.academia.edu/35495485/The Most Litigious Countries in the World, July 10, 2021)*

Writing for Forbes in 2013, conservative commentator Carrie Lukas lamented, "Americans have so long been saddled with a litigation culture that it's hard to recognize the full weight of its effects." With the infamous McDonald's hot-coffee case as the foster child, one 2016 poll, according to the Wall Street Journal, found that 87 percent of voters said there are 'too many lawsuits filed in America'. (Jay M. Feinman, July 23, 2020, The Washington Post).

Some Google facts about lawyers and litigation:

"The study, released by the U.S. Chamber of Commerce's Institute for Legal Reform, indicates, nationwide, the cost of litigation hit $429 billion, or 2.3 percent of U.S. gross domestic product in 2016 (instituteforlegalreform.com)"

Civil Filings. Civil case filings in the U.S. courts increased 3 percent (up 9,279 cases) to 286,289. Federal question filings rose 2 percent to 150,936. (2020)

The United States has more civil litigation than any other nation in the Western world.

It's estimated that over 40 million lawsuits are filed every year in the United States and the total number of registered lawyers exceed one million, with a population of 331 million.

The United States of America is the country with the highest number of lawsuit as % of population. However, many of these are civil cases under tort law (i.e., class action suits against tobacco or drug consumption) not an individual suing another individual or entity or a perceived injustice. (Google, February 2021)

Lawyers advertise everywhere: signs, buses, and all other media. Their advertisements spur individuals to raise their conflict to legal instances so they can sell their service. People here and there are arrested.

The intensity with which individuals seek to force the compliance of the other will be equal to the revenge and righteousness used.

Contrary to what it should achieve, when law seeks to protect all individuals from all trespasses of others, it achieves trespassing all. Americans constantly ask if they are breaking any laws. An excess of laws would therefore be an exaggeration of society. The American citizen introjects law as a way of living and becomes an enforcer toward his neighbor.

In countries with little law enforcement, law abiding citizens live quite a peaceful relationship with authorities knowing that law enforcement happens only to real criminals. However, little law enforcement gives room for unpunished crime and trespasses; individuals live in fear of being vandalized or trespassed by fellow citizens.

In America, law abiding citizens are liable to break laws by mistake or omission, so they comply with certain fear. This is why Americans are so prompt to threaten. Law enforcement will provoke resentment if felt unfair, and unfairness can be a subjective appreciation.

Marriages break up, the fight for properties begins, and lawyers make money out of the dispute. Lawyers secure their income on the properties they are fighting for. If the couple runs out of money to continue the fight, lawyers will keep the property. It is an economic machine that keeps money going around. This does not happen in other countries; lawyers will not secure their income on the assets of their clients.

Schools and Law Enforcement

The news in the radio (15 February 2021) informed about a police officer who was based in a high school in Kissimmee, Florida and subdued a teenager female to the ground. The girl was being violent to a peer and needed to be stopped. The video was shown in social media. The police chief, Christopher Mall, who has been dealing with these issues for 15 years, was asked a moral question: "Wouldn't it be better to teach students to behave correctly rather than to house a police officer in the school? The answer was 'Yes, we have said it for many years'."

School and home are the sanctuaries where children are educated and taught moral values to eventually become the adults that will run the country. Morality is to be taught by example and these sanctuaries are to be kept away from the atrocities of the world. To bring law enforcement to them is a contradiction. Since law enforcement is the failure of social reasoning, to invite it is to neglect reason.

A teacher teaches, a prefect corrects, a policeman subdues, a military eliminates. Do we want children to merge and reproduce the system, or do we want them to transform and improve it?

Schools need to prevail as loving and caring environments and at the same time be corrective. The problem is that entertainment and media aimed to older children and teenagers is demoralized. Schools then do not know how to cope with this problem and invite law enforcement, which only makes things worse. The solution is not to have policemen searching for arms in schoolbags; the solution is not making arms available to children.

The morality crisis is preposterous and it has to be attended. Because it is not being attended, more law enforcement is needed. The contents of entertainment and media need to be regulated. As life is the most important value for humanity, entertainment that is oriented toward abusing, killing, and other forms of antisocial violence needs to be reoriented.

On the other hand, America has gone beyond ethicality. Education is not lacking in ethical behavior (it is lacking in morality). Children know too well what is good and what is not. If parents were to fail in teaching so, the entire system will take care of educating them. America has gone so far by making law enforcement greater every day, that it is becoming 'unethically ethical'. When all is enforced, all actions are watched and everyone is afraid. When people are afraid, they become violent and thus more law enforcement is needed.

There is an ambivalence of wretched morality derived from entertainment, and an ethicality fostered by education and law. The result is a morally confused citizen.

The Confused Righteous Citizen

The individual may come to believe that he has the power of the State, as we all introject what is taught to us. Instead of negotiating a solution to a conflict, the individual rushes to punish. This is why individuals cancel, sue, retain payment, and threaten—all symptoms of unforgiveness. However, an individual cannot be a judge and a party; this is a principle of law.

An American believes that when he is trespassed (which may be a misinterpretation of what the other needed to do according to his circumstances) he is entitled to become a judge and punisher. One thing is to be an advocate of law and promote the rule of law, and another thing is to become a judge. However, since punishment is derived from a rather revengeful response (law takes lawful revenge over trespassers by principle) the punishment itself in the hands of the 'trespassed and hurt' individual may be a trespassing action itself. Therefore, if the individual believes he is doing 'good' by punishing, he may actually be doing 'bad' or 'worse' without realizing it. Or, if he misunderstands an action that was not intended to trespass him, his response can become the first and only trespassing action.

The contradiction is that since society has successfully taught Ethics to all citizens; they not only follow the law but also become judges and enforcers. The ethical individual becomes unethical by retaliating with an eye for an eye action. An eye for an eye ruling was the practice before the republic and law existed. Therefore, an excessive practice of ethics has gone beyond ethicality, sending us back to historical times. At the same time, since America is the country with most lawsuits in the world, retaliation is thus doubled. The punisher may punish on his own and with the aid of the judiciary system. This is a cause of anger in society.

As the nature of law enforcement is violent, when the individual becomes an enforcer on his own, he punishes violently. Confused individuals think they are entitled to punish regularly. The 'better' citizen an individual is, the more law abiding and punisher he becomes. Therefore violence is praised. On the other hand, dominance understood by the American as his rightful prerogative inherited from the British Empire, can turn human relationships into a battlefield. Individuals engage in emotional wrestling powered by dominance. One consequence of dominance is oppression. The oppressed individual will not be free.

The ideal citizen is law abiding. The more laws, the more guided and restricted his actions are. The more restricted he is, the closer he is to perfection: an unsentimental, uncontradictory, flawless citizen. If he fails to be perfect, he will be corrected.

The butler in the film The Shining (Stanley Kubrick. 1980), more than a butler plays the role of a moral guide to Jack Nicholson; he is actually his conscience. The butler is an (deranged) enforcer of rules who cannot tell the difference between social behavior and family relationships which should be founded on tolerance and love. The butler 'corrected' his own family and entices Jack Nicholson to 'correct' his own. The butler is characterized with a British accent, suit and a tie of course, thus suggesting that male chauvinist puritanism, law, and law enforcement are inherited from the motherland. Jack Nicholson is the metaphor of family behavior enforcement in a deranged world.

The all-legislating state breaks human closeness and separates individuals. It denies human fallibility. Separateness is more intense in American society. The perfectionist individual is unhappy by definition; he will clash with things and events.

"As the modern individual cannot be angry at the State, he is angry at his fellow citizens." (Byung Chul Han, The Palliative Society: Pain Today, 2020)

"The real freedom is to live in peace with the other". (Ikram Antaki).

Since Ethics delimits freedom and the exaggeration of ethics derives in fear of the other, peaceful relationships are slowly drifting away.

The combination of two sources of confusion may affect some individuals in society. On one hand, there will be a confused morality derived from immoral violent entertainment, and on the other, the individual will assume that he has the legal right to punish.

To be fair, it ought to be said that the American judiciary system is not only vindictive but is also forgiving. It forgives through community work, short stays in jail and fines, classifying a fault as a misdemeanor, and pardoning a trespasser.

Antidote 1

Educate differently. Rely more on prevention (moral education) and less on correcting results (law enforcement).

Educate society to reason and care for the other. Practice more forgiveness and less unforgiveness.

Contradiction 2
Can Guilt and
Freedom Coexist?

To exert guilt upon the other has the purpose of correcting him. The guilty individual is expected to apologize, learn, and correct.

Contradictorily, guilt is a manipulative, highly effective, and cheap resource; it may be exerted without explanation and is likely to abate self-esteem.

Grant Wood 'American Gothic'

"Guilt is the enemy of liberty."
(Byung Chul Han)

Guilt is the preferred resource to punish the other. Guilt is violent, guilt blames, guilt finger-points and reduces the individual; guilt is oppressive. Guilt can also be used with the purpose of manipulating another person. The person that exerts guilt becomes a victimizer, while the recipient of guilt becomes a victim. Being a victim or a victimizer are the roles to act in the play called 'American Life' at the Law and Order Theater Company.

Americans internalize the imperial attitude inherited from the British Empire in their way of life and thus act imperially with the other, trying to exert dominance. This dominance is positive when in the form of leadership generates development, but destructive when triggered by conflicts.

Guilt and dominance go hand by hand. He who exerts guilt dominates the other and at the same time justifies dominance. It works for individuals and works for nations. Because being a victimizer brings plenty of gains, like the liberation of resentment (unresolved anger), the angry society then becomes a *vindictive society*.

Victim–Victimizer Relationships

When an individual feels abused, he will voluntarily play the role of victim. When in anger wants to take revenge, he will play the role of victimizer. It is not easy to escape from this symbolic old-fashioned British duel with pistols. Any individual can play these roles, from a citizen to an authority.

Individuals will profit from exerting guilt. When being a victimizer, all advantages are on his side. When being a victim, there are two ways out: apologizing and repairing, or fighting back.

Since being guilty is a disadvantageous position, individuals will do all they can to avoid being finger-pointed. They will do the right thing or do what is safe to do, or blame the other. They will be over-conscious of the other.

Because circumstances may be adverse and it is only human to err, it is inevitable to be a victim of the other. Sooner or later, no matter how perfect individuals try to be, they will fail.

Crisped social relationships trigger the victim-victimizer conflict. The victim (the good) has been trespassed and becomes then the victimizer (the good and the bad) leaving everybody blind in this eye for an eye, tooth for a tooth dynamic.

Victims become victimizers. Molested children will become child molesters. Bullied children will become bullies. There is an introjected bully in many Americans, who will be ready to bully when the occasion deserves it, that is, if such occasion were to exist at all, morally speaking. For many, it is a question of who wants to get even with the world when the opportunity appears. Anger and pride are the fuel; low self-esteem is underlying.

Adults teach their kids to behave through guilt. When children grow up, they become victimizers by exerting guilt, not only to their own kids, but to everybody. Many

Americans do not realize that they are vindictive because it is the system of values that they were raised with.

Anger does not always find the correct avenue, so these questions have been posed to describe anger management:

- Is the individual communicating the anger to the person that caused it?
- Is his anger proportionate to the cause inflicted?
- Is the timing of his anger release different from the time it was inflicted?
- Is the reason of his anger the real reason behind the anger he is feeling now?

Individuals with poor emotional intelligence may feel angry to the casual passerby. As no country in the world is yet utopia, there will always be citizens left behind that ought to be comforted and reincorporated to the mainstream of limited liberty and opportunities. The dream of every country is that the percentage of left behind citizens is small and will grow smaller.

The uncovered haters through Trump's regime, unveiled a poor anger management culture in a higher percentage of citizens than it would have been expected. The real causes of hatred will depend on each individual's personal history. This history is comprised by their family background (nurtured or neglected) and by social insertion (included or segregated).

Vindictiveness condemns what it interprets as evil or imperfection of the other. Attachment to this belief creates constant conflicts, making life about pride. Triviality and pride are opposites. Triviality is to understand that something that looks important, when observed, reveals its unimportance.

Law is about honor, truth, and righteousness. For law, nothing is trivial; matters are either allowed or not allowed. Law restores the pride of the infringed individual and takes away the pride of the infringer.

Law enforcement needs to humble up with non-violent people because bullying citizens creates fear and violence. Vindictiveness is in charge of the American way of life today and the unveiled haters are a proof of it.

> The film 'The Tenant' (Roman Polanski 1976) portraits in the new tenant the person that faces social rejection as the neighbors expect him to perform the life of the former tenant. The new tenant is pushed to be alike his predecessor and is rejected by his neighbors. Even the coffee shop across the street serves him the food and cigarettes that the former tenant used to order. It is the dilemma of pertaining versus being pointed at. It is by vindictiveness that the new tenant is cornered and ends up becoming the former tenant. The former tenant had committed suicide. The new tenant (acted by Roman Polanski himself) commits suicide also, thus making a statement about the *vindictive society*. Since he is not free to be himself, he cannot be.

In America, immigrants try to pertain, especially when there is discrimination involved. The sooner they merge in society, the more secure they will feel. After having been pointed at, some will become more American than Americans and may even catch up with the anger of other individuals. The fancy car, informal clothing, fast food, and above all: a new and strange relationship with doing the right thing, where they become law advocates and finger pointers, trying to stay on the side of the victimizer, rather than the side of the victim. First generation immigrants may disapprove of new immigrants after a few years in the country.

The victimizer has power over the victim. Once he is able to inflict guilt over the victim, he can obtain all sorts of gains. This only happens because American culture responds submissively to guilt.

In order to be safe, there is an infallible resource: to isolate. But even then, friends and family will finger-point the individual for isolating. Still, it is better than being exposed. When the other is perceived as a threat, solitude is safe.

All this tension and fear soon find an escape valve when the other is the one that fails. The individual will respond in the scale of his own shame. The angry citizen will blame, threat legally, dispute bills, write long disappointment letters, and so on.

Social relationships, that go from driving in traffic, walking in a parking lot, to meeting class mates or peers, teachers and bosses, customers and customer service people, are opportunities to coincide or clash, as in any society. The way each society deals with these daily events makes this experience different from one country to another. Some cultures will be more prone to non-verbal communication, such as smiling or nodding, while other cultures may trigger a riot of verbal expressions. Americans solve their differences through guilt.

- A male customer is being taken care of by a sales girl in a stone and tile store. He tells her what he wants for his home and what his home is like. He takes off to take a look at another product on his own and leaves behind the sales girl. Another customer who was queuing to be taken care of asks the sales girl a question and she takes care of him. The first customer comes back, gets angry at her, and feels abandoned. He goes to the counter and asks for the manager. The man on the counter (a first-generation immigrant) was aware of the situation and offers that he can take care of him instead. The customer says, "No"; he says he does not want to repeat everything to him. He insists on wanting to see the manager. The man on the counter also insists on taking care of him and the customer finally agrees.

To me, who was watching all this happen while I was queuing in a different line, there was no right or wrong, only circumstances, fortuity, and fallibility. The customer made a choice when walking away and the sales girl made a choice while he was gone. The ethical issue here is that the customer was about to act vindictively by complaining about her to the manager, with the intention of causing her harm. The size of his anger was not proportionate to what had happened.

Another day, I paid at the supermarket with a credit card. It did not go through. The cashier inflicts guilt upon me with his unfriendly non-verbal communication. I pull out a second card, it does go through and the cashier shows appraisal with his words and an extremely soft tone of voice.

Suffering a guilt disorder, as result of living in a *vindictive society*, can be healed through self-compassion.

Victim-victimizer relationships are perversely enjoyed. If Angela makes Bruce feel guilty, and relishes upon the exerted misery, Angela is entitled to satisfaction. If, however, Bruce does not show proof of guilt to Angela, she will hit harder the second time. This is why individuals are so prone to offer an immediate apology: to stop a triggering rage, the introjected rage of God (see Chapter 6).

A self-confident personality, with high self-esteem, may shield from the pointing fingers. However, if an individual does not feel shame for trespassing, he becomes a social misfit. Since all extremes are out of range, self-exoneration on one hand and unforgiveness on the other are both anti-social behaviors.

Love, on the contrary forgives all; family and close friends will bring comfort from these everyday momentary troubles. If family and friends were to be unforgiving, happiness will not be easy to find for an individual.

The American educational system educates through guilt. The film 'The Wall' depicts British education in the postwar. As of today, individuals 55 and older were educated in the postwar. The input I receive from children and teenagers tells me that education has not changed that much nowadays in terms of guilt infliction. Education has to evolve. Otherwise, society will only repeat itself, tied up in guilt-fear-violence dynamics.

A sign in a park reads, "Screams and shouts go beyond the boundaries of this park, be considerate of your neighbors". I do not remember reading a sign like this in other countries. Should the American play in silence, or shush his child and teach him not to express his feelings? My house is in front of this park. What a joy it is to listen to kids playing, laughing, and yes, screaming and shouting! What a joy it is to listen to teenagers playing also! Even more joyful it is to listen to adults playing; many of them have forgotten how to play.

- A customer was asked to buy his own grout so the company could install tile for him (the company made a mistake and missed to by the grout). The customer, a 70-year-old man, on the verge of crying, totally above himself, shouted at me, "Why should I have bought it? I had to go to Home Depot. It was not my fault, it was not my fault!" I stood dumbfounded and felt many emotions. He was right of course and was making a fair claim; he deserved an apology which I gave to him. But he was also behaving like a 5-year-old in need of a hug and an 'I love you'. I was not the person he was looking for to say it. Parents and teachers do not know how harming and lasting guilt infliction is for a child.

American society creates this misbehavior because an extreme amount of guilt is spread out since early childhood. Society has not found yet a better way to convince citizens to act morally. Guilt has been the easy way: it is expedite, effective, does not cost a penny, and when inflicted at a young age, becomes powerful. Naturally, there is a guilt disorder called IEGS (Inappropriate and Excessive Guilt Scale), that causes depression and there is a special therapy for it. *(www.goodtherapy.org/learn-about-therapy/issues /guilt)*

Inflicted guilt is inherited from The Old Testament, as I explain further on in my research about the religion brought to America by the British new settlers: Protestantism (Contradiction 6).

In my everyday life as a provider of products and services, not being able to fulfill customer expectations like a perfect machine creates all sorts of disappointments. An employee showing 15 minutes or an hour late, with or without reason, mistakes happening during installation, unforeseen events, and defective or mistaken products delivered to us: the list of possibilities is endless. Trying to reduce and control these variables on our side becomes our goal, of course. Suffering the consequences of human error from the customer's point of view is uncomfortable in a society so perfectionist. Intolerance and violent behavior invade business relationships. Threats and guilt infliction are everyday resources. On the contrary, whenever things go well and the work is done correctly according to the customer's expectations, most customers will be supportive, polite, and very grateful.

We learn to behave through guilt and consequences. The latter is inevitable, but we do not know how to teach without diminishing self-esteem. So we create ambivalent education going from guilt to appraisal, sometimes not giving enough time for the child or the adult to assimilate either one, when the opposite feedback happens.

Nonverbal communication by means of a gesture or a posture can be as powerful. When the victimizer exerts guilt with nonverbal communication, it is your task to fill in the blank. However badly you were treated is how you will talk to yourself. But if you have worked on healing yourself or you had supportive and loving parents, the blank may remain empty.

The Defensive Approach to Vindictiveness

No one wants to be in the inevitable position of being guilty. Therefore the individual will do whatever is necessary to avoid being blamed.

Aside from the usual 'the blame is on you, not on me', not out of a vain impulse to not take responsibility but due to a quite profound and justified intent to avoid being a victim in a blameful society, the individual also takes other routes to avoid vindictiveness.

One way may be to speak up and point out a mistaken situation in order to avoid a major damage (and then be blamed for not communicating it). This is good and helps to keep the system working and being reliable.

Another way is not only to point out a mistaken situation, but to point directly someone who will be the trespasser and therefore the sinner, turning the informer into a saint. This dynamic is also functional in terms of making the system work. However, good faith and good judgment need to prevail in order to avoid betrayal. It will also require reparation to the 'sinner' through a sincere apology for having communicated his fault. Betrayal is a cause of anger.

If this reparation is done beforehand, "I need to inform that you made a mistake in order to avoid a bigger damage…" the informer will be assertive and in no way will betray. He also gives the trespasser the opportunity to be the informer himself, thus avoiding him irreparable consequences (loss of job, bad reputation, lost opportunities, lost friends, money, and so on).

If the informer gives the trespasser the opportunity to inform, he will miss all the possible gains of being a saint (a promotion, recognition, the dream of a salary raise, and so on).

To be an informer brings more gains than not to be one. That is why betrayal is so common. As betrayal is implied, when the fault is trivial, the 'saint' may be doing more wrong to individuals and society than the 'sinner' himself. In my daily job, betrayal is a daily matter. Contractors will speak badly of other contractors, trying to be on the right side of the story, fighting to become the saint, probably because on the previous job they were pointed as the sinners, all symptoms of guilt infliction.

When a victim of denunciation experiences that he has been betrayed without enough reason, he is likely to become a victimizer in the future.

Julia bought a toy poodle puppy for her three-year-old daughter and so the girl and the puppy grew up together. At age 16, the poodle became blind and deaf. The daughter told her mother that the time had come to put the dog to sleep. This brought some conversations in the family about life and death, the right to live, and living beings not becoming trashable. The conversation migrated to humans and euthanasia. Bella was the poodle's name, she was in no pain, and she would eat with appetite and sleep most of the day. Bella was taken to the vet regularly and kept clean. Even at age 16, she looked like a puppy.

One day, a customer came to the office and strongly recommended to put the dog to sleep. Her input was thanked, but in no way a stranger was in a position to determine the life or death of a loved pet. It is true that Bella was old and her quality of life was not good, but Julia was waiting for nature to simply take its course.

One week later, the customer came back to pick up her order. On her way in, she started a conversation with one of the employees of the company and asked him to do a service for her (without going through the company, thus saving money). She then asked quite startled why the pet had not been put to sleep yet.

The next day Humane Enforcement of San Diego (can humanity be enforced?) showed up. An armed female officer went into the office without knocking, searched for the dog, found it, and left a 48-hour notice to show a vet appraisal in order to decide if the pet should live or die. Two days later, she came back and took Bella.

The feelings are mixed and it is a controversial situation. People can discuss over the issue and may not come to an agreement. But anyway we see it, the customer betrayed. She betrayed Julia in two different ways: by meddling and interfering in the privacy of a family-pet relationship, and by hiring an employee directly.

When an individual wants to become an informer, there must be a very good reason behind because in a law enforcement society there will be consequences. This means that the informer will indirectly damage a person and the people that surround her for the sake of doing the right thing. The informer takes the attribute of being a judge and indirectly, of acting as law enforcement. In this particular case, the pet was causing no harm to anyone and was slowing dying as part of life. The right thing becomes debatable as it depends from whose point of view it is right or wrong: Julia, the customer, society, or the daughter. Human exceptionalism considers that the dog has no standpoint in this debate.

The modern citizen cannot take pain; society eliminates it through pain relievers and neglects it as it believes that the right thing is to be happy. Happiness and pain cannot be separated, as both necessarily coexist…The lack of empathy toward other individuals makes them an object of consumerism. (Byung Chul Han, the Palliative Society: Pain Today, 2020).

The customer could not stand the pain of seeing somebody else's dog's going through old age. The customer acted according to her own created morality. She found Julia guilty of keeping an old dog alive, took the role of a judge and ruled.

On the other hand, the capitalist society trashes whatever ceases to be useful. Had the customer respected God's will toward life and death, she would have done nothing about it. Had she understood life through spirituality she would have respected life and nature. She acted like a consumer, who on her way in, used her money to seduce Julia's worker. Had she acted ethically, she would not have tried to hire directly an employee that has cost time and money to insure and train. Surprisingly, Julia states that this situation happens regularly; customers will hire directly her employees.

Going back to Bella's humane enforcement, another ethical question is raised. How close are societies to 'enforce humanity' to people? Will your neighbor be able to inform that your mother or father is not fit to live? In other words, can human exceptionalism toward animals extend to younger age exceptionalism toward old age? It is not only about euthanasia, it is about the power of being an informer and to betray.

As everyday life may occur lovelessly in the guiltful law enforcement environment, individuals may suffer from extreme separateness. Rather than filling up loneliness with nurturing love, resentment shows. A friendly and short verbal exchange with a cashier in the supermarket may seem meaningless, yet it may be the oxygen needed.

There is a third position in this victim-victimizer relationship: not being either one. Now and then I read the word 'forgiveness' in different contexts around town. In a Catholic Sunday mass in San Diego, the message given in the sermon was 'I forgive you'. There is an incipient claim in American society for forgiveness.

The film Mrs. Doubtfire (Chris Columbus, 1993) depicts a blameful environment where Robin Williams, a loving father, is misunderstood by his wife, later on by his own children and society. He is guilty of being a jobless though talented actor and a bit senseless but passionate father immersed in the perfectionist reality of his wife's world; in consequence, Sally Field divorces him. He has a hard time finding a job in the TV industry as an actor. The film creates the metaphor of Robin Williams having to go through a long process of daily disguise and make-up to earn forgiveness. Half of the story is about Robin Williams asking society to forgive him. He finally masters his career, gets back his right to meet undisguised with his children, and recovers respect from Sally Field. Forgiveness is the happy ending to the story.

Forgiveness is the happy ending to all stories.

Antidote 2

Forgive, be emphatic and compassionate; understand that we are all fallible.

Avoid feeling like a victim, avoid being a victimizer. Be respectful, trust.

Love, coincide instead of clashing with the other.

Discern between doing the right thing and betraying.

Compliment the other.

Contradiction 3
Is Capitalism the Best
System in the World?

"There's class warfare, all right, but it's my class, the rich class, that's making war, and we're winning." Warren Buffet

In Capitalism, the individual is free to work and be successful; the ceiling to his success is his own limitations. Salaries are sufficient and individuals enjoy a stable economy.

Contradictorily, wealth is massively accumulated in a few hands, new technologies are unemploying individuals, salaries went down and the lower class has a hard time pertaining to society.

The republic provides laws, limited liberty, and equality to citizens. Democracy allows for citizens to choose their politicians, to participate in policies, and to be represented. Capitalism provides work and money. What could go wrong?

Robert Skidelsky gives us a historical view of economics and its distance from ethics and morality, being the laws of economics only those that favor the creation and accumulation of wealth…Arithmetic is the only measure to economics whereas ethics and moral belong to another universe, so to speak. Capitalism was the price we had to pay to progress. Love of money is ethically bad, but it is the means to achieve the good; by creating abundance it will allow future generations to live wisely and agreeably and well… (Ethics & Economics, How & How Not to Do Economics with Robert Skidelsky, 1983)

Four decades have passed since this statement and that future of wisdom, agreeability and wellness of life is not in the horizon yet. Moreover, it would seem to be moving away. It reminds us of Socialism being the painful first step before getting to Communism, the new utopia, one century ago.

Many decades ago, for Hegel and Kojève, Capitalism and liberal democracy were a success.

- Thus, capitalism and liberal democracy are configured like the great organizational instances to which the spirit (the culture for Hegel) has arrived in its long historical via Crucis marked by the struggle and the search for power, but also by reason and calculation: there is not a higher order. It is, in fact, a thesis that is not only held by Hegel but by the Soviet Alexandre Kojève (1902–1968) whose interpretation of the

Stuttgart philosopher had a great influence on the intellectual circles of France between the two World Wars…

- It is Kojève and not Hegel, who affirms that 'we have reached the end of history because life in the universal and homogeneous state is completely satisfactory for its citizens. The modern liberal democratic world, in other words, is free of contradictions' (Dr. Sergio Pérez Cortés: Hegel: Religion and Free Thought)

Endless intellectuals and philosophers have discussed the contradictions of Capitalism, such as Wendy Brown, Gilles Lipovetzky, David Harvey, Robert Reich, and Enrique Dussel. The belief that Capitalism has brought down poverty by one billion people, has been debated by John Edward's research.

"The UN's sustainable development goals, launched in September, are set to use the $1.90 line to measure poverty. Why do they persist with this implausibly low threshold? Because it's the only one that shows any meaningful progress against poverty, and therefore lends a kind of happy justification to the existing economic order. If we want to stick with a single international line, we might use the 'ethical poverty line' devised by Peter Edward of Newcastle University. He calculates that in order to achieve normal human life expectancy of just over 70 years, people need roughly 2.7 to 3.9 times the existing poverty line. In the past, that was $5 a day. Using the World banks' new calculations, it's about $7.40 a day. As it happens, this number is close to the average of national poverty lines in the global south. So, what would happen if we were to measure global poverty at this more accurate level? We would see that about 4.2 billion people live in poverty today. That's more than four times what the World Bank would have us believe, and more than 60% of humanity. And the number has risen sharply since 1980, with nearly 1 billion people added to the ranks of the poor over the past 35 years." (John Edward. Capitalism Has Not 'Lifted Billions Out of Poverty' Nor Has Economic Growth 'Benefited The Environment', The Specter of Communism, Dec. 13, 2021)

Ambition within Capitalism is the breeding ground for success, investigation and development. Capitalism is the economic system that best functions, where even the less wealthy individuals agree with it as long as they have their basic needs satisfied. Nevertheless, below a certain level of income, the lack of abundance creates anger. The consciousness of inequality confronts individuals. Capitalist income per capita seems to have become an exaggeration of America, and since Americans are not happier or better educated than other developed or underdeveloped countries, a few questions rise. John Hike brings up some questions about this:

"Instead of pushing poor countries to 'catch up' with rich ones, we should be getting rich countries to 'catch down'.

"What does this mean for our theory of development? Economist Peter Edward argues that instead of pushing poorer countries to 'catch up' with rich ones, we should be thinking of ways to get rich countries to 'catch down' to more appropriate levels of development. We should look at societies where people live long and happy lives at relatively low levels of income and consumption not as basket cases that need to be developed toward western models, but as exemplars of efficient living…

"Yes, some of the excess income and consumption we see in the rich world yields improvements in quality of life that are not captured by life expectancy, or even literacy rates. But even if we look at measures of overall happiness and wellbeing in addition to life expectancy, a number of low- and middle-income countries rank highly. Costa Rica manages to sustain one of the highest happiness indicators and life expectancies in the world with a per capita income one-fourth that of the US.

"In light of this, perhaps we should regard such countries not as underdeveloped, but rather as appropriately developed. And maybe we need to start calling on rich countries to justify their excesses…

"Even at current levels of average global consumption, we're overshooting our planet's bio-capacity by more than 50% each year. In other words, growth isn't an option anymore—we've already grown too much." (John Hike, The Guardian, September 23, 2005)

There would be then an amount of wealth and expenditure that allows people to be fulfilled, and an excess of wealth and expenditure beyond which societies are no longer fulfilled.

> "True happiness is to enjoy the present, without anxious dependence upon the future, not to amuse ourselves with either hopes or fears but to rest

satisfied with what we have, which is sufficient, for he that is so wants nothing." —Seneca.

There should be nothing wrong about money; it serves an exchange purpose. It is popularly known that money is not happiness, and without money there is no happiness.

Money Rules

Presumably, money is obtained through work and the harder a person works, the more money he will make. However this is not completely true. Money can also be inherited, obtained through investments, revenues, rental of properties, and so on. Some ways to obtain it seem easier or more advantageous than others. This will also create inequality in the lifestyle and therefore will produce anger.

For Romans, to have a job was servitude. The ideal happy citizen would not work. Idleness was a virtue, a privilege, more than a sin (sloth).

Today, money rules over morale and individuals. Money is more than individuals; it is a being with its own 'intelligence' that subjugates individuals and countries. Capital has its own laws and will make the rich richer or the poor poorer overnight. This will also create anger.

In the film 'In Time', salary is metaphorically represented by earning time as a way to continue living. Employees work full time and queue on Fridays to get one more week of lifetime transmitted to a biological gadget inside their wrists. If they don't work and do not earn time, they will drop dead. People that are not part of the system get more hours to live from relatives or friends who kindly pass it on to them wrist to wrist but they in turn need to recover it through means different than working. Wealthy people carry many more decades than they want to live in their wrists. The metaphor points out how in capitalism people depend on their salaries to survive. As Wendy Brown states, people are only 'one salary away from living in the streets'. The film unveils the crude reality as in one of the climaxes a mother and his son run toward each other because she is running out of time. The mother uses her last seconds of life to reach his son's wrist but drops dead one step away. (In Time, 2011, Andrew Niccol)

So is happening today when cancer medicines are not affordable, medical insurance has reached its limit, and governments fail to provide healthcare. In this and through many other ways not less dramatic, people die without money.

In the context of global warming, those who speak on behalf of mother Earth are confronted with the 'make money-no make money' question.

Sustainable Design is defined as product design that is beneficial to:

1. Companies
2. Earth
3. Society
4. Consumers

If a sustainably designed product does not meet these four conditions, it is not sustainable. In other words, a sustainable product may help to save the planet, but if does not make money, it is useless. This is understandable of course, and controversial.

Banks have been allowed to take away unpaid properties leaving individuals in poverty, or insurance companies are allowed to always bill but not to always reimburse or reimburse insufficiently; being sick is a sin that has to be disclosed in order to lose the benefits of being insured. Banks lend the money that does not exist and profit from interests. Most citizens in capitalist countries will acquire loans of fake money, so to speak, bringing it to existence when they pay the interests with their work.

The anger that Capitalism entails goes beyond having not. The social individual loses a purpose and cannot pertain to society when segregated economically.

> For the capitalist individual, there is a loss of purpose and fatigue because of struggling much and achieving little. (Gilles Lipovesky)

Because the republic was intended to procure an adequate environment to the citizens, its laws were created to apply equally to all. When society is unequal, the republic loses this attribute. America, the world's role model of democracy and capitalism, is being questioned for inequality.

> The neoliberal structure of society and governance are giving a new shape to human beings, where citizens are no longer political citizens but economic sources; governments do no longer rule companies and care for the well-being of citizens but to be an economic force to back up the companies. Politicians are no longer praised for achieving a superior and harmonic society, but are praised for achieving a booming economy. (Wendy Brown, Undoing the Demos: Neoliberalism's Stealth Revolution)
> Populism reaches the unhappy individuals in society, the real victims who not having achieved economic success in the capitalist environment, resent society. (Ethics of Liberation: In the Age of Globalization and Exclusion, Enrique Dussel, 1973).

Team work is enhanced because it produces more money, while togetherness as opposed to separateness is avoided. Togetherness, understood as fulfilling happiness derived from human contact is yearned in the adult world.

The strong competition in capitalism, introducing money as the sole prize, and being it limited to those who obtain it following the rules of the system, turns individuals into rivals. If an employee, your peer is your adversary; either you covet his salary or he covets yours. If an entrepreneur, your customer is your adversary; you need his money. If a purchaser, your supplier is your adversary; if you pay him less your boss will reward you. If you suffer from an injury, be 'smart' for there is someone you can sue.

Linda, a teenage girl was driving her car to high school. When the cars were queuing to enter the parking lot, she got distracted with her cell phone and hit the car in front of her. She only released the brakes; no dents did ever show on either car. The car that she hit (pushed) was driven by a mom and her daughter was on the right front seat. The mother got out of the car complaining of severe pain on her neck while her embarrassed daughter tried to talk her out of the farce. The mother claimed neck injuries for thousands of dollars. Insurance companies had to solve the issue.

Only law can stop us from fighting with fists and teeth. Words such as 'delinquent, lawyer, and court' turn business relationships antisocial. As money is the unique goal, conflicts will always be oriented toward paying less or paying more, causing anger in society.

Stephen, a Scandinavian immigrant, paid a thousand dollars insurance for his two cars. After he and his wife retired, they sold one of the cars since they could manage with one only; they were willing to save money. He informed the insurance company and the next bill came again for a thousand dollars. He complained and was told that the insurance was calculated based on the risk and the drivers, not on the number of cars. "We have to deal with a lot of crap to live in this country," he concluded.

Consumers are enticed to sign contracts with a few clicks from a smartphone. Later on, when disappointed they try to cancel, it will take letters, long phone calls to a robot, and might even have to wait for a year. If they miss to cancel on the given date, another year will run. Governments overlook unethical behavior. This is another cause of anger.

Individualism is narcissistic, for it cares for nothing except oneself, his own job, his house, his family. (Giles Lipovetzky, L'Ere du Vide.)

Many couples share their money and understand it as common means to live life and achieve things. Other couples hide money and keep their income, savings, and properties separated, making the less wealthy one to live margined within marriage. When money becomes the predominant value for one of the partners in a couple, or when one partner mistrusts the other, love is dismissed. Trust is the foundation between partners. An unequal relationship is not a loving relationship but a one party's domain.

Capitalism needs to be moralized. Americans behave nice to each other when a transaction is starting to take place (money for a product/service). Unsatisfied customers, with or without sufficient reasons, are vindictive and try to obtain more through claims, or try to get away without paying. Customer service departments serve as a scapegoat to contain the anger of a perfectionist society. The unsatisfied customer syndrome is an American epidemic.

A nineteen-year-old is the manager of his father's ice cream business in downtown San Diego. He and his girlfriend often serve ice cream to customers and share the same opinion. "I do not like my job because people often get angry at our fancy ice cream dishes! How can someone be angry at an ice cream?"

The capitalist individual considers his money as his own property. He is attached to it and when making bigger expenses, he does not really want to let go of it. He takes on a posture of 'you owe me' even though he has already received the good/service. The capitalist individual will be vindictive and will demand perfection in exchange for his money, which in essence to him, is perfect and complete, compared to the imperfect good/service he is receiving. He fails to remember that he received money through delivering an imperfect good/service. For him, it is a one-way street.

Money loses its exchange quality and becomes carnal, a body part that is painful to release. Many customers will use dissatisfaction and imperfection to pay less money. On the contrary, spiritual individuals are prone to let money go more easily, as they can detach from it and understand that money is only a means. If the 'neoliberal morality' is to make money, and all licit activities that produce money are allowed, society is then money driven, and not value driven, with law and law enforcement acting as the Fire Department. Capitalism and Ethics do not go well together. Capitalism is governed by greed, need, and mathematics. Ethics and morality belong to another realm.

Paul owns several properties and requires performing maintenance when tenants leave. He developed woodworking skills and decided to build cabinets and millwork to repair his own houses. When a friend of Paul saw the good quality of his work, he asked Paul to build cabinets for him. When the job was finished, his friend recommended Paul and sooner than later Paul had enough customers to rent a small facility, he hired a few employees, bought a CNC, more woodworking machines and started a company.

For ten years he was a successful cabinet maker that received an extra income and kept himself busy while still taking care of his own properties. One day, a customer with a big home hired Paul, and a remodel of a few hundred thousand took place. The vindictive homeowner started to become invasive towards Paul's company; he gave orders to the employees and changed instructions of the job following his own decisions and not following the contract. The job itself, now run by a homeowner and not by a professional, lacked good planning and in consequence, lacked quality. This went on for weeks without Paul being able to stop it; soon the homeowner "fired" Paul from the job and paid directly to the employees. When the homeowner stopped all payments to Paul, Paul filed a lawsuit asking for the balance to be paid. The homeowner in return filed a lawsuit against Paul saying that everything had poor quality and was carried out incorrectly. Now Paul faces a three hundred thousand lawsuit.

Disappointed by the customers, his employees, and a lawsuit, Paul shut down the business. Now that he will have to sell his CNC and equipment for peanuts, he also has to deal with the anger against an economical system that lets people down, in spite of thousands of laws meant to guide social relationships. His employees lost their job, Paul lost his company, lawyers are earning money, and a vindictive homeowner made a good deal wrong inspired by perfectionism and greed. Is it necessary to write a few dozens of new laws or is there something else that society is missing?

Prosperity courses link the love for God with prosperity. It is true that prosperity and faith in God are linked, because when individuals behave correctly socially, inspired by a religious morale, love will drive their actions. It is in giving that receiving will happen. So giving love in the form of a good service/product will in turn bring love in the form of money. However, to feel love and act lovingly is easily said but not easily done, especially when the individual has to spend money to give love. The selfish natural inclination of the individual does not want to give much. Only naturally generous people, or people that consciously make the effort to act generously can achieve being part of this cause-effect love per love commerce, so to speak. When people and companies give love in the form of a product or service, the world will be a better place.

Capitalism and Education

As higher education becomes inaccessible to many families, universities and colleges have found a way to keep in business: to lend tuition money to the students. The young professionals will merge into society with a debt, and many of them will be paid low salaries. They will spend valuable years paying their loan, instead of creating their patrimony.

> In John Grisham's the Rooster Bar (2017), four law students foresee that their salaries will not be enough (the college they attend educates them poorly) to pay the tuition they owe. They are afraid of the world and fear drives their antisocial actions. Their gigantic debt seems unpayable and one of them commits suicide in his last semester. In consequence, his three friends leave school, blame the university and the system for his death, and mourn by evading their future responsibilities. They practice law without being licensed and profit illegally from a typically American opportunity to make money (a company is sued, the judge sentences it to pay every customer a restitution) and the students get a commission for every customer to be reimbursed. They fake hundreds of names, knowing just enough law to avoid it and fight the system. The ethical dilemma posed is realistic. Though dramatized in fiction, it is a reality of higher education.

Intelligence and education are no longer a guarantee of success in the capitalist world. Uneducated individuals who are skilled enough for doing business will be rich. This discourages young people from studying and parents from going through the hardship of paying for higher education. This can be a cause of anger as individuals may no longer be able to link effort and study with money. Since going to college and excelling as a student is not necessarily producing wealth for the individual, new generations find other ways of making money. Young ones have a hard time choosing a profession, especially when jobs are changing and robots and computers execute tasks. People are asked to be software proficient (mind-finger-keyboard skills) rather than humanly proficient (mind, heart, spirit). The profession loses importance to a skill. Michael Sandel explains meritocracy in the neoliberal economy.

"Meritocracy encourages individuals to take responsibility. Merits will make individuals achieve a better social position, meaning that training, education, and hard work will produce money.

"However, meritocracy fails to explain that rich families tend to produce rich descendants, while poor families tend to produce poor descendants. Thus, meritocracy serves more as a justification of the neoliberal world, rather than the solution for social mobility.

"If the success of individuals is a result of their own doing, then so is their failure. Selfishness of society will again prevail over the fate of those who are less fortunate. This logic makes meritocracy corrosive to society because it cancels empathy and generosity. It seems that the winners of the globalization need to convince themselves that they deserve being at the top. Meritocracy is not a remedy against inequality, it is a mere justification." (Sandel, Michael J. The Tyranny of Merit: What's Become of the Common Good?)

Meritocracy will then fit in the *vindictive society* because the wealthy ones deserve their success, while the poor ones deserve their failure. That was the discourse of monarchies. There is no real change in centuries of class warfare, only new wording. Bullying of rich kids toward poor kids continues.

Capitalism is in need of being moralized. Education shall focus more on human values, and less in money making skills and values, provided we grow consciousness. We need a fresh understanding of common good. Since Church is losing adepts for several reasons, the question that rises is who will teach morality?

The Unreached American Dream

People need an explanation as to why they cannot reach the American dream. This dream is only attained by few, relatively speaking. Big success, big business, and accumulation are a result of talent, but also of fortuity. Being at the right place with the right amount of money, doing what is needed to be done by real successful reasoning and/or by chance, finding the right partner, employee, or consumer are all variables that account for success or failure. To gather the money and coincide with the circumstances needed to start a business takes effort and years. There is only one chance to make it right because if the money is gone, the next opportunity may take years to reappear.

It is a capitalist misbelief that whoever does not achieve the American Dream is because he is not capable enough—all circumstances ignored.

> When we were raised, our parents were able to support the family with one salary, higher education was not as expensive as it is today, and the State would provide with services that no longer provides for. All is different in the neoliberal world and the amount of time and work invested do not necessarily produce what it used to produce. (Wendy Brown, Undoing the Demos: Neoliberalism Stealth)

The American Dream has a component of happiness and quality of life, inasmuch as what individuals understand by 'dream'. The physical environment (care for nature, well planned urbanism, the quality of products and services, high income, and so on) is well achieved in America, as in other developed countries. The psychological environment is not one that enhances fully a dream-like happiness because of the stated contradictions.

The American Dream would then be limping. The wellness of the physical environment is enjoyed by individuals and extended to a majority of the territory and citizens, while the anger provoked by the vindictive society procures a rarified psychological environment where happiness is somewhat missed.

Extreme Wealth

The extreme accumulation or loss of wealth is not limited and little legislated. This is contradictory, in a society where so many activities are legislated. Robert Reich addresses these issues consistently.

> Tax cuts to the wealthiest damage the country because the government needs this lost income to distribute it among the less successful individuals, by means of healthcare, ending poverty, infrastructure, and more. (Robert Reich, 'What if We Actually Tax The Rich?' YouTube, April 1, 2021)

Unrestrained wealth accumulation is as harmful as any unrestrained human activity. A single person is free to accumulate more wealth than a small country's annual budget, while another person is free to lose all overnight (i.e. gambling, divorce). This lack of regulation is one cause of the failure of capitalism. Capitalism may not be failing, but is failing individuals. Unrestrained wealth and loss of wealth are exaggerations.

> Wendy Brown quotes Thomas Picketty about unruled capitalism '…a thing about when they (capitalists, millionaires) are really left to themselves, is that they generate capital accumulation at a much greater rate that they generate growth… (Allowing for an) increasing

concentration of wealth at the top, increasing impoverishment across society and a fairly stagnant economy, a form of neo feudalism… (Rob Johnson interviews Wendy Brown, May 25, 2016)'

There is no limit to wealth, but there is a limit for salaries. These contradictions are allowing for a new rusted socialism to reappear when we had thought it gone forever.

People are valued by their money, not by their human worth. If somebody Googles 'how much worth is (a name)', the answer is a number and a picture of a happy individual: the more zeros, the 'better' the person is. Millionaires become celebrities that people look up to. Celebrities are evaluated by money, which should be private information, inaccessible and unimportant to the public. Capitalism and media have made it important and public.

Extreme wealth is also a very strong driving force that is used to create even more development, technology, and money. When a billionaire accumulates such capital, there is a question that rises: would he be able to change the conditions of poorer societies, not by charity of course, but by transforming social structures? Or, on the contrary, should he go on pushing wealth and be more successful? Citizens in social media take two opposite positions toward billionaires. They either treat them as deities because of their ability to achieve, or they are treated very badly for the same reason. Extreme wealth is either idolized or despised, but always envied.

Jose Saramago, Portuguese writer and recipient of Nobel Prize in Literature in 1998 states:

There is a certain perversity and immorality in wealth. Wealth can come from work, from inheritance, or by simply belonging to a wealth family…What does not make any sense is that we should be doing something to redistribute wealth… (and we are not). Some years ago the US sent an apparatus to investigate the rocks in Mars, everybody was surprised. To me, it is immoral to find it fun to learn what the rocks are like in Mars if I allow at the same time people in Earth to starve to death; it is senseless…It is obscene that given the circumstances for all humanity to live a dignified life, millions must starve to death or die ill. It happens in Africa, in Latin America, how can we allow for kids to live in the streets…? (YouTube, Mistoria, 25 December 2020)

The argumentation is simple. It deals with hierarchy of values. Saramago is not arguing against science or technology. For him, it becomes futile to investigate Mars when we are lacking basic things in Earth. It would be like buying a luxury car when the house is lacking heating in the middle of winter.

Monopolies are increasing; the capitalist machine needs to be humanized because dehumanized individuals suffer from mistaken social interactions.

Love cannot be accumulated; it expresses itself only when given and received. A person cannot be rich in love if he keeps it to himself. So is with money when it is correctly understood.

Antidote 3

Discern between value and price. Life is about people, not about money.

Choose your values well as money is related only to price.

Money is a means. Money comes and goes, be generous. Do not steal by paying less.

Contradiction 4
Americans Are Powerful; What Are They Afraid Of?

Citizens will ideally reason and follow the law. Contradictorily, citizens also follow the law by fear. Fear generates a violent biological response; in consequence individuals become violent citizens.

The Scream, Edvard Munch, 1893

"Freedom is not worth having if it does not include the freedom to make mistakes." (Mahatma Gandhi)

Fear drives American society. Fear of getting too close to someone, fear of not being safe, fear to trespass rules and laws, fear to fail at work and school, fear of not making enough money, fear of being pointed at, fear of the other.

Fear is a biological response, a reflex, not a thought. *(The culture of Modernity, Claudio Alvarez Teran. https://youtu.be/mf58ziqjw4e)*

Fear of Punishment

Let us define the word 'punishment' by using Google dictionary (Google, September 24, 2021)

> Punishment: the infliction or imposition of a penalty as retribution for an offense.
> "crime demands just punishment"
> Similar: Penalizing, punishing, disciplining, retribution, damnation, chastising, chastisement.
> "She assisted her husband to escape punishment for the crime."
> Similar:
> Penalty, discipline, correction, retribution, sentence, vengeance, justice, judgment.
> Rough treatment or handling inflicted on or suffered by a person or thing.
> "Your machine can take a fair amount of punishment before falling to pieces"
> Similar: Battering, thrashing, beating, thumping, pounding.

The bright side of punishment would be, according to this definition: retribution, correction, discipline, justice. The negative side of punishment is: beating, vengeance, damnation.

Children are punished in school and inflicted with embarrassment and fear since a very tender age. I remember the public scorn of being sent to the corner of the classroom against the walls for the rest of the class, just to mention one of the correction methods. Is this the best we can do as society? For some, psychological damages last forever.

In a way, to inflict fear over people is successful because it serves a purpose.

The Legal Purpose of Punishment

Deterrence prevents future crime by 'frightening' the 'defendant' or the 'public'. The two types of deterrence are specific and general deterrence. Specific deterrence applies to an 'individual defendant'. When the government punishes an individual defendant, he or she is theoretically less likely to commit another crime because of fear of another similar or worse punishment. General deterrence applies to the 'public' at large. When the public learns of an individual defendant's punishment, the public is theoretically less likely to commit a crime because of 'fear of the punishment' the defendant experienced…

Incapacitation prevents future crime by removing the defendant from society.

Rehabilitation prevents future crime by altering a defendant's behavior. Examples of rehabilitation include educational and vocational programs, treatment center placement, and counseling.

Retribution prevents future crime by removing the desire for 'personal' avengement (in the form of assault, battery, and criminal homicide, for example) against the defendant. When victims or society discover that the defendant has been adequately punished for a crime, they achieve a certain satisfaction that our criminal procedure is working effectively, which enhances faith in law enforcement and our government.

Restitution prevents future crime by punishing the defendant 'financially'. Restitution is when the court orders the criminal defendant to pay the victim for any harm and resembles a civil litigation damages award.

(open.lib.umn.edu/criminallaw/chapter/1–5-the-purposes-of-punishment/)

The intention of law enforcement is to bring peace to society and trust in the government. The contradiction is that broadcasted punishment inflicts fear to everybody.

Law enforcement agents use deterrence as a resource. They are taught to use a specific body language that makes citizens fear them. We learn as children that a friendly policeman is an extension of our parents who in the streets will protect us from a bully or a thief. As adults, we find out that he has become a bully that we may not want to get that close to. Many of them will still be friendly and they ought to be thanked for that, because one of their functions is to communicate that they are to be trusted, not only feared.

Deterrence has psychological effects that can harm society in general, especially if one third of the population has a criminal record.

The Fearful Individual

Through ethics and law, the State has achieved a highly restrictive society, and a lonely one. Criticism and finger pointing are at a rise. The solution is not more enforcement but more ethicality.

I do not remember people saying the phrase 'get home safe' when I lived in Tacoma back in the 70s. I was still living in a cocoon, like many children. I heard 'get home safe' for the first time when living in New York in 1992. Since there had been so much crime in the city, I thought that it was a local expression. When I arrived to San Diego in 2021, I heard people say 'be safe' when saying goodbye. San Diego is a city where there is little crime, shootings can happen anywhere in the country, no tornados, no extreme weather. Law and order have taken care of providing safety to individuals. If there is no apparent reason to feel unsafe, I wonder what this outspoken fear responds to.

> "Through the first five months of 2021, gunfire killed more than 8,100 people in the United States, about 54 lives lost per day, according to a Washington Post analysis of data from the Gun Violence Archive, a nonprofit research organization.

That's 14 more deaths per day than the average toll during the same period of the previous six years." (The Washington Post, "2020 was the deadliest gun violence year in Decades, so far, 2021 is worse." Reis Thebault, Joe Fox, and Andrew Ba Tran, June 14, 2021)

"From late May until the end of June 2020, roughly 20 million people in the United States participated in demonstrations over the death of George Floyd, as well as Breonna Taylor, another Black body, among many, perceived to be discriminatorily targeted and killed by police…systemic racism was finally classified by many as a public health crisis." *(Pandemics and protests: America has experienced racism like this before Jennifer D. Roberts, June 9, 2021, www. Brookings.edu/ blog/how we rise)*

Needless to say, shootings and racism add fear to society. Ethnic groups are discriminated regularly. In 2021, it has been the turn for Asian immigrants (so the news reveal), and Afro-Americans, of course.

Aside from these direct, evident causes, in everyday life there are other symptoms of fear. Americans want to double check, to be reassured, to be on the same page, confirm an already confirmed appointment, confirm anything one, two, three times, as if doing so will avoid the unavoidable to happen, only to be surprised or deeply disappointed when it does happen. On one hand, this rigorous follow up gets things done. On the other hand, a flat tire will still occur, no matter how many times they confirm. This fear and lack of faith in the other, or God, or the universe only tenses up relationships and thus recriminations happen every day when something fails. Recriminations and double checking are communicated by any means available. Communications go on during the day, after hours, 6:30 am, Saturdays and Sundays. There is no respect for privacy. People expect to be answered and may be resentful when not answered to.

Fear is stronger than love and people will turn their back on others for the sake of law. People are separated by the state and torn by fear.

> The film Brazil (Terry Gillian, 1985) is staged many decades ahead in England. Jonathan Pryce performs an idealist who falls in love with a woman (Kim Greist) believed to be a terrorist. He dreams of her as an angel and warrior of liberty, the liberty that is not available in the system he lives in. He breaks several laws of the (British) authoritarian system trying to help her.
>
> Michael Palin impersonates a good friend of Jonathan Price that works for the government. Jonathan asks him for help in order to find and protect Kim. Michael lends Jonathan his own uniform that will open the doors of government buildings for him. He advises to make good use of it. Jonathan offends again when he breaks into an office searching for her file in order to make it disappear. He breaks the law as an act of love.
>
> Jonathan and Kim eventually meet again and run away from the punitive system and the city, fleeing to encounter love surrounded with nature, and free at last. When they are caught by the police, he is

taken to a torture room, all his trespasses were recorded. Blindfolded and soon to die from torture, he is surprised to recognize the voice of his torturer: his close friend Michael Palin.

The British judiciary system gave birth to American judiciary system. Both countries experience rigorous law systems.

To report suspicious or unlawful activity is encouraged. If the judgment of the citizen is wise, he will prevent a crime. If his judgment is incorrect, someone will suffer from his report. The authority will investigate until it has no more doubts. If an individual did commit an illegal action, he will be punished with a cause. If it was a mistake, he will be traumatized. Teenagers often do things that are not well seen by adults, like drinking, screaming, or driving carelessly and they will be reported. Misdemeanors will be punished as such, and the happy and festive young American may turn into a fearful and sometimes resentful adult, who forty years from now, may be the one who files a report against a noisy teenager. Since finger pointing is praised, and being finger pointed at is dispraised, society turns vindictive rather than empathetic.

Children have birthday parties and invite their class mates. If one of the kids has an accident (kids have accidents because it is part of their nature, not a fault of whoever shares his home with them), the parents of the hurt child will threaten and in some cases sue the homeowner. A friendly society becomes a fearful society. What would seem to be an innocent gathering of friends is not.

The evaluation method where a student rates a teacher or an Uber driver rates the passenger who in turn rates the driver, has created a change in society. George Orwell's Big Brother is not only restricted to a coercive state. The Big Brother is us. (Orwell, George. <u>1984</u>) Society, through exerting guilt and punishment, was successful to teach and allow individuals who used to be evaluated, to evaluate. We are all watching each other; staring may have now an added purpose. Every individual carries a camera and the means to report.

The cell phone has become a new ID, through which control is exerted. Through our cell phone, we leave the traceable activities of our daily life. Every place where we interact will ask for our phone number. So if an individual feels he has done something 'incorrect' the traces of his cell phone will make him fear.

The opposite of fear is faith. Have faith in God, in the unknown, faith in the existence and equilibrium of universe, or even faith in yourself if you are atheist. To have faith is to have certainty in uncertainty.

> I am in a home with a young realtor. She is in her late 20s. I am in my late 50s. We need to look at a bathroom that needs remodeling. The bathroom is inside a bedroom and we go in. The bedroom is rather small, with a king size bed. We are quite close to each other. As she opens the bathroom door, a puppy sneaks out. In the 21st century, we are in trouble. (In the mid XX Century, it would have been a straight forward situation: grab the dog, close the door.) I have the impulse of closing the

bedroom door in order to trap the dog inside the bedroom, but as I am about to latch the door, I think twice and stop: I fear she may sue me for sexual harassment. She wants to grab the dog but she stops also, she fears she may be sued for pet abuse. She moves away, so I move away, the dog runs out of the bedroom. She then runs after it, calling silently because she fears upsetting the home owner who may point her finger at her. A quick yell to the owner would have solved it, "Hey Mrs. Davies, can you please come downstairs and grab your dog!" So there we are for 10 minutes, waiting for the untouched puppy to come to his senses and freely walk back to the bathroom. I thought it would never happen. We gave away discussing the bath remodel, of course. This is how dysfunctional American society is becoming, a fear driven society.

I asked an engineer to read this story; he told me he is an avid book reader. His house is nice, above average in San Diego. It has a swimming pool and some huge stones, about the height of a kid, between the pool and his back fence. This is what he told me.

"I totally agree with you and I feel the same way about it. And I understand you were not able to speak about the bath remodel. The other day some kids jumped over the back fence and were having fun climbing the big stones by the pool. The only thing I could think of was that they were going to sue me if there was an accident, so I ran and asked them to leave."

What struck me about his story was that as he spoke tears started to flow from his eyes and his face turned red. He had to pull out a napkin and clean them because he was not being able to see me. I felt his empathy, despair and sadness. Our own neighbors have become our potential enemies. Little kids are to be avoided.

> A woman clicks on a home improvement website and we receive her information and a request to contact her. A $60 is charged to our account and we make a phone call. She answers that she did not request a consultation and hangs up the phone. She is afraid. We call again (we need her to cancel the consultation so we can get our money back) and she threatens to sue us if we keep on harassing her. Now she is in panic. It is hard to explain to her that we have her name and number because she requested a consultation as she is out of her senses; she speaks all the time and does not listen. She was probably scrolling on the website and clicked on the phone screen without noticing.

Scams and crime take place over the phone; people rarely take calls from an unknown number unless they are expecting a call, which generates uncommunication and deceit. Twenty years after the first virus appeared in the internet, we still have to be careful of opening unwanted emails since we can become the target of different ways of crime. These are other causes of fear.

"Trust no one," said President Trump to his children, and when made public, it was broadcasted to the country as an endorsed belief. Certainly mistrust is not his own idea, but he reinforced the debatable belief of Protestant predetermination (refer to chapter 6).

Trust is the opposite of fear. Individuals do not trust each other, because there is a constant fear that the other will fail or will be dishonest. The individual will quickly conclude that the other has failed, because he was firmly expecting it. He will blame the other and make him pay.

Trust is to be nurtured in society, not mistrust. Mistrust may get things done, but it makes people lonely and vindictive. Trust does not need to be a synonym of failure. When moral values are taught, people are to be trusted. However, if mistrust prevails, the emotional relationship between individuals will suffer and will give room for abuse. Contradictorily, mistrust would then become the prelude of failure, because a violent response is being predetermined. What we most fear is what we attract.

Trust the other as you trust yourself. Believe that the other has the same capability as you have to care for important things. Trust in the goodness of the other, as there is goodness inside of you. Communicate all you want and need. Then let go and wait for the results. Do not communicate a list of threats. And most importantly, do not abuse the other, because you may be the only abusing party; respect and accept. "Trust, but double check" is still based on mistrust, but at least it is a better attitude than 'Trust no one'.

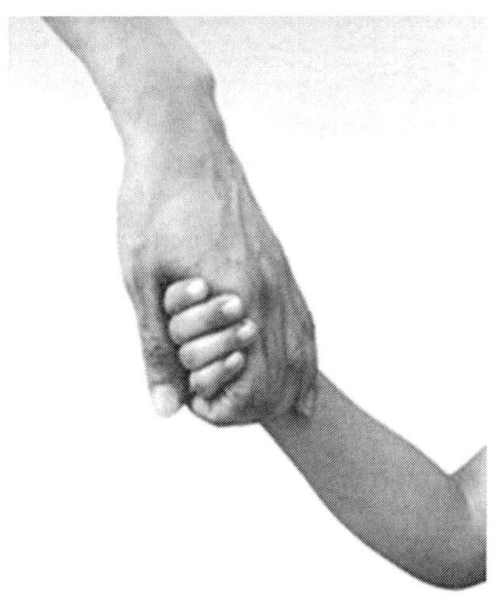

Antidote 4

America: educate and trust your citizens.

Citizens: educate your children with love and moral values and then trust them.

Contradiction 5
America Procures a Peaceful Environment, but Is the Culture a Violent One?

Children are raised safely in pristine homes and schools, while violent entertainment is chasing after them.

The superhero sublimates violence in a fictional reality.

American TV, film, and computer game industries have excelled in violent action plots, using all the resources available to be visually abundant. On one hand, American society morale is based on the Calvinist condemnation of total depravity (sinfulness, as described in the next chapter, page 105), and on the other hand, fictional total depravity (refer to page 105) is welcomed by entertainment laws.

Along with sex scenes, violent scenes left in the past the power of insinuation. As these industries became explicit (a few boundaries have not been broken yet) and transparent:

> "The excess of transparency has become pornographical" (The Society of Transparency, Byung Chul Han, 2012).

It would be naive to believe that there would be no repercussions in human behavior. TV, videos, and film educate through stories and are massive entertainment. Children and teenagers, while cocooning in a 'safe' environment, are exposed to violence when they are not ready, that is, if society were to ever be 'ready' for it. So much has been said about this for decades, that there are no words to describe this malpractice of society.

In a society with such abundance of laws and restrictions, violence would seem to have been exempt of censorship. The films Scarface (Brian di Palma, Oliver Stone, 1983) or Pulp Fiction (Quentin Tarantino, 1994) left behind the paradigm of insinuation and subtleness. Senses are targeted, intelligence and ethics are neglected. Censorship became a bad word and film shooting debauchery took its place. It is not about bringing

Puritanism back, it is about saving lives; it is about not putting bloodshed in the minds of children and teenagers.

Mass shootings happen every week and keep a continuous flow of criticism to the NRA. Violence learned from early childhood dehumanizes and normalizes homicide in the context of a Second Amendment never ending debate where millions of dollars in opinion of many Americans, are behind. A country with over 700 military bases in the world and with a military state of mind has to deal with military kind violence issues within its borders.

If arms were banned and violent plots were discouraged and allowed to exist with limitations in media and entertainment industries, who would then want to join the army? The military should not rely on the violent penetration of the entertainment industry, if that were the case.

Back in 2006, I went to Blockbusters in my home town and picked up a family film to watch with my 9- and 7-year-olds. I chose Spiderman. I don't know why I had this strange idea that Spiderman was a film for little kids. Was the name deceiving? In the 70s, I watched Spiderman cartoons in TV. It is an adult film with violent scenes. Failing to read the Blockbuster classification had really bad consequences. When the enemy in a flying motorcycle with protruding spades penetrated the body of his victim (bleeding was shown), my 9-year-old son stood up in extreme alert, turned pale and lost his balance. My 7-year-old twin girls did not react at all, which is not less intriguing.

We cannot avoid our children from facing evil experiences in life; moreover we have to give them the tools to overcome them. But there are ways, intensities, and moments.

Action films often have a protagonist that solves the conflict of the plot. Many times, the protagonist is a superhero, with or without superpowers, but with attributes that will make him to be admired by the audience.

The Superhero

Superman, Captain America, and other superheroes have penetrated the culture of Americans. Dressed with the colors of the American flag there is no doubt to the rest of the world that the superheroes have an American identity.

Law enforcement officers solve real life conflicts and become superheroes. Not only that, there is a superhero in every citizen, and this is not common to other nationalities or countries. The cultural penetration of the superhero is such that most kids play with this idea; the game goes on when they become adults.

The super hero, who was humane when stopping a train from hitting a car driven by a person, saving a baby, or rescuing Luisa Lane from Lex, has dehumanized because what is to be restored today is law and order, while people are dispensable. The villain has to pay, not anymore by going to jail as in plots of the mid XX eth century, but by being massacred, thus neglecting humanity. Rambo killed 83 in his last film, nearly an average of one homicide per minute. The superhero sublimates violence in a fictional reality.

Not all the superheroes are involved in physical violence, but they may exert emotional violence. The superhero can be the boss, the employee of the month, the dad, the single mom, the passing by citizen, or a policeman. Society venerates the super hero and prompts all citizens to become one. In solitude by nature, the super hero earns his position by his deeds; once he gains authority he may impose punishment upon others.

> The film 'Employee of the Month' (Greg Collidge 2006) shows us the relationships in a work environment where the current super hero of the store (a charismatic and agile employee) will not allow an emerging super hero (the new employee) to appear. All this happens under the supervision of a feeble boss, in a small town anywhere in the US. The pretty girl is portrayed as the prize, thus dehumanizing love and making women appear as objects.

Law enforcement agents are expected to be super heroes, restoring law and order and forsaking individuals.

> I went running by a lake in a hot day. I ran for about one hour. It was humid; there was no sweat evaporation, waves of hot air struck me as I ran. I should not have gone running on a day like that, but it was Sunday and it was my pleasure to do it. My body temperature rose to a point where I needed to

cool down drastically. Taking off my shirt under the shadowy trees did not work. I felt sick; I knew I was close to having a heatstroke.

I dove into the lake although it is forbidden to swimmers; it is a reserve of clean water for human consumption. Contradictorily, it is allowed for motor boats (water pollution by oil and debris picked up from the roads is likely to happen) and for fishermen sitting in their inflatables for hours. There are fish and ducks, so the water has to go through a cleaning process before it is drinkable.

Within minutes, a park ranger approached, just as my body was recovering its temperature. With the attributions of a cop, he relished in his power of imposing guilt. He asked me to come out. I knew that opposing to law enforcement may be interpreted as a felony and I have seen videos of men, women, and even children subdued. My body was in no physical condition to be subdued.

As I walked out of the lake without complaining he must have felt frustrated. "Do I know that the lake is a reserve of drinkable water and that I am polluting it? Do I understand how bad it is for me to do that," and so on. Would he have enjoyed seeing me handcuffed and next thing go home proudly to his wife and kids for dinner?

The point is that he did not ask. He did not empathize with me. A man in his fifties that dives in the lake most likely knows how to read and should have a special reason for doing so. He might have asked and helped me in some way; I needed to drink water badly and was feeling sick. My car was 200 feet away and I did not have the strength to get to it. I am at least 20 years older (and wiser) than him. Respect for age is not in the vocabulary of law enforcement. It is man against man: in order to protect somebody from being hurt, somebody needs to get hurt. The former is an unknown possibility; the latter is in front of you.

I would have preferred a flying superhero with a bottle of chilled water and a few oranges, rather than a superhero saving the lake. And I would not have wanted a 911 call either, bringing in paramedics to study my vital signs and declaring that I should not run around the lake in that weather, becoming the emergency call of the area and probably billed large amounts of money.

The value of preserving my life was more important to me than following the lake rules. I knew that if I mentioned I was close to having a heat stroke, he could call 911. All I needed was to cool down for a few minutes in cool water, for Christ's sake.

"Values have a hierarchy. The most important value is to preserve human life. This value prevails over all others…" ('Ikram Antaki, Toward a Citizen Ethics', You Tube, 2000)

I also understand that it was my own perception to be afraid of law enforcement (was it because of successful *deterrence*? Page 70) and that I could have been mistaken. Had I told the park ranger my situation he might have become emphatic…I opted for not taking that risk. I was not in the mood to engage in a conversation like this:

The introjected policeman, "You shouldn't have…"
Anybody, "Yes, but you know, the reason behind was…"
The introjected policeman, "Anyway, you shouldn't have…"
Anybody, "I know, but I needed to…"
The introjected policeman, "Well, next time, before you…"

These conversations may seem repetitive and tiresome since we all know the beginning, the middle, and end of them, yet they give sense to rules in society.

Another Sunday, I had the chance to become a superhero myself!

I am running in the park. A dad pays attention to his child and the skate board slowly running astray stops in the middle of the narrow trail where I am running. The introjected superhero inside me urges me to say, "Hey! Somebody is going to get killed with that skateboard. You should pay attention to it. Unbelievable! If you don't pick that up, I will …" But I simply run around it: I forgive and say nothing. I do not stare at the dad or at the child vindictively. As I am passing by, the dad notices, runs for the skateboard, and apologizes. *Errare humanum est.* No need to apologize to me. So I miss the opportunity of becoming a superhero, save the planet from tripping over a skateboard, making a child feel miserable—and I only feel very happy about it! I feel ashamed of myself having produced those bitter thoughts.

The Country of Exaggerations

"According to Aristoteles, the supreme value is the midpoint between two vicious exaggerations. For example, an excess of courage can provoke death. The lack of courage can also provoke death. The lack of generosity can be destructive in a family. The excess of generosity can also be destructive in a family." (Ikram Antaki, Toward Citizen Ethics, Part II, Masterclass)

America is a country where exaggerations happen. Abundance and excesses have led to some or many exaggerations. This is why America has the largest number of inmates, law suits, and lawyers. The Vietnam War was little understood back then as it is now, having caused an exaggeration of deaths and expenditure. America has the best sport performance in the world which often involves a damaging, stressful life for athletes. It also has the biggest amount and wealthiest billionaires, the biggest companies, the greatest armament (until China superseded it), while some people believe that moving to Mars is the solution to the world. This is why if you question law enforcement you may end up handcuffed. When kids go to college, they go to another town or state, causing big expenses to their families. Drug abuse in youth is overspread; rehabilitation from drug addiction is common. Consumerism is always on the rise. This is why vindictiveness is overwhelming and money prevails over almost anything. Mass shootings happen regularly, arms are sold in supermarkets and violent racism never seems to come to an end. Many bills to pay a service, a tax, or a product are notified with a threat. Health care is so expensive, slow, bureaucratic, and inaccessible for those not covered by insurance. There are super-size food options, extra bonuses, and scams chasing us. The challenge for this society would be to find the midpoints, not the exaggerations.

> A film documentary shows an experiment. A man has his health tested and the results show that he has excellent health. He eats healthy food and exercises regularly. He decides to take his three meals in the same fast food restaurant and every time he is asked to order 'large' or 'extra' he agrees. After 30 days, and walking not more than two and a half miles a day, he goes back to have his health tested. He is told that they do not know what he is doing wrong, but if he keeps on doing it, he will die. (Super-Size Me, Morgan Spurlock, 2004, independent film)

The Culture of Violence

America inherited imperialism from the motherland as a way of understanding the world. When the colonial America was founded in 1607, the British were in the process of ruling 24% of the planet and 23% of world's population under the Empire. When World War II ended, the reverse process finalized and most of the remaining colonies became independent. In consequence, the natural heir became the United States, taking advantage of its military intervention, imposing global rules to a weak Europe, Russia, Japan, and China who were the rivals at that time.

An empire cannot exist without dominance, nor can a superpower. Dominance is exerted through different avenues, such as military, economic, and rhetoric. All three if exaggerated, become violent.

Violence in American culture has spread out to social relationships. Contradictorily, the purpose of law in a republic is to achieve a peaceful and happy society. Violence is not to occur in social relationships which should be peaceful.

American society has been teaching violence for decades: from Tom and Jerry, The Lone Ranger (a TV series from 1950, performed by Clayton Moore, is a fictional masked former Texas Ranger who fought (killed) outlaws (native American Indians) in the American Old West with his Native American friend, Tonto (a traitor). The character has been called an enduring icon of American culture. Google, September 15, 2021) and all police and thieves series, to computer games and cartoons with all sorts of bloodshed. People are entertained with lawbreaking stories and are contradictorily punished when they act accordingly.

We have seen in the screen unimagined ways to commit crimes and the ways to get away with them. Disturbed minds find the inspiration they need in 'fun' entertainment.

The number of lawsuits, convictions, and murder are higher in America than most European countries. The ethical question is, can any society, including American society, be improved, not only by enforcement but by education? Enforcement is only a consequence, and a very expensive one. Actions are needed upon the causes.

> The Truman Show (Peter Weir 1998) depicts the perfect politeness in a pristine society; unfortunately, it is staged for a TV show, in a movie, with the intention of fooling a man. In fact, it is a rude politeness because it is faked. We would all like the world to be perfect, if it were possible. In the story, utopia is unreachable by definition, and whoever believes in it is an innocent Truman.

Some Americans wish the world was like Disneyland. A futile wish if observed superficially, but it's a deep and valid claim of transforming the country into a truly (and not apparent) friendly society. Disneyland is a fantastic environment where individuals forget that they live in the real world.

To be an American is to react with violence to what is perceived as a trespass of the other. The contradiction is that a violent response in itself is a cause of violence, not to mention that the perception of the individual may be biased by his own reality. The violent response of a person that 'feels' has been trespassed, is not a reaction; it is a cause of violence.

As society has not found a better way to solve differences, it is through violence that issues are solved.

To exert guilt is the number one resource. 'You should have…and you didn't', as opposed to 'I should have…and I did not'. There is a third position: let us evolve and move away from the 'should haves' that were not. We are fallible; we do our best, and now let us solve the problem.

The culture of violence needs to become less violent as a first step. Entertainment stories need to change. The villains are not to be eliminated but reinstalled in society; the individual should be praised again because of being an individual, and not disposed of when being fallible.

A Parable of Forgiveness

The parable of the Lost Son exemplifies loving versus violent reactions. **Luke 15**

The Parable of the Lost Son
11 Jesus continued: "There was a man who had two sons. **12** The younger one said to his father, 'Father, give me my share of the estate.' So he divided his property between them." **13** "Not long after that, the younger son got together all he had, set off for a distant country and there squandered his wealth in wild living." **14** After he had spent everything, there was a severe famine in that whole country, and he began to be in need. **15** So he went and hired himself out to a citizen of that country, who sent him to his fields to feed pigs. **16** He longed to fill his stomach with the pods that the pigs were eating, but no one gave him anything. **17** "When he came

to his senses, he said, 'How many of my father's hired servants have food to spare, and here I am starving to death! **18** I will set out and go back to my father and say to him: Father, I have sinned against heaven and against you. **19** I am no longer worthy to be called your son; make me like one of your hired servants'." **20** so he got up and went to his father. "But while he was still a long way off, his father saw him and was filled with compassion for him; he ran to his son, threw his arms around him and kissed him." **21** "The son said to him, 'Father, I have sinned against heaven and against you. I am no longer worthy to be called your son'." **22** "But the father said to his servants, 'Quick! Bring the best robe and put it on him. Put a ring on his finger and sandals on his feet. **23** Bring the fattened calf and kill it. Let's have a feast and celebrate. **24** For this son of mine was dead and is alive again; he was lost and is found.' So they began to celebrate." **25** "Meanwhile, the older son was in the field. When he came near the house, he heard music and dancing. **26** So he called one of the servants and asked him what was going on. **27** 'Your brother has come,' he replied, 'and your father has killed the fattened calf because he has him back safe and sound'." **28** "The older brother became angry and refused to go in. So his father went out and pleaded with him. **29** But he answered his father, 'Look! All these years I've been slaving for you and never disobeyed your orders. Yet you never gave me even a young goat so I could celebrate with my friends. **30** But when this son of yours who has squandered your property with prostitutes comes home, you kill the fattened calf for him!' **31** 'My son,' the father said, 'you are always with me, and everything I have is yours.' **32** But we had to celebrate and be glad, because this brother of yours was dead and is alive again; he was lost and is found."

Google answer for 'What is the meaning behind the prodigal son?'

"In the story, a father has two sons. The younger son asks for his portion of inheritance from his father, who grants his son's request. This son, however, is prodigal (i.e., wasteful and extravagant), thus squandering his fortune and eventually becoming destitute" (Google, May 14, 2021)

The online explanation of this parable stops after the introduction of the story and misses to explain the story. "…eventually becoming destitute" would seem to be the end of the story, which becomes then the final judgement from the Protestant point of view. On the contrary, this is where the story begins.

I will paraphrase therapist Graciela Escalante. She treats perfectionism as a type of neurosis, and uses this parable as a psychological foundation to understand this pathology. A philosophical analysis might draw different conclusions, and so would a religious one.

The parable is about two perfectionist sons. One son asks for his will to be given to him before his father dies. The other son stays with his father. The former spends all the money in pleasure and sin, while the latter works loyally by his father's side. When the sinful brother repents and comes back moneyless to his father, the older brother condemns him and his father.

The sinful son got lost in the way. He ceased to be good and sinned. He repented out of famine and misery. He told his father he was not worthy of being called his son anymore; he was not able to forgive himself. Perfectionists are not able to forgive. He asked to be taken back as a servant. He could have gone some other way and never come back, but he went back to his father.

God, who is infinitely good and is the father in the parable, acts forgivingly and sees not the mistakes of his son, but his repentance. The father does not neglect him, nor calls an authority to take him away; he receives him with the best clothes, food, and jewelry. We know that this child may fail again, and the father will always offer him mercy. Mercy is defined as the forgiveness received from God when not deserved.

The older son is a perfectionist that will not forgive the mistakes of his sibling nor his own. He is haunted by his own self-righteousness, he is intolerant and miserable. He resents not being free and to be by his father's side. He resents not having enjoyed his youth thoughtlessly. He is angry at his father and blames him for showing love to 'this son of yours', no longer recognizing him as his brother. He is not content living in goodness by his father's side. He works for his father without love as a driving force, and therefore resents work.

He became the victimizer in the parable, since he has been the never righteous enough person—nobody can be. So when the chance came, he blamed his brother who had blatantly enjoyed life.

The father had missed so much the prodigal son that he thought he might have lost him forever. When his son came back, *Love* in the form of compassion changed the father. *Love* also changed the prodigal son in the form of self-compassion. Simultaneously, the touched father still showed love to his older son and assured him that the properties were still his. The father gives the resentful son back his brother when saying, "This brother of yours"; the father will one day be gone, but the two siblings will be brothers until death departs them.

However, *Love* did not touch the resentful son and he remained as the sole victimizer, violent and unable to forgive his own beloved brother, the brother whom he shared his childhood with. He is all alone, the only miserable and resentful soul that does not enjoy the party held for his brother's return.

Many Americans behave like the resentful brother, blaming the other, telling the father, the boss, or the sheriff, about the other's trespasses. They expect the other to receive punishment. They want the other fired, blamed; moreover, they will feel satisfaction over it. This happens because this is the way we have been raised in school, and sometimes at home.

American society is so ready to blame, and so unready to forgive. It is an unforgiving society where an individual may not even forgive his own children. The average American, if triggered, is merciless in the daily events.

It is not important if you believe or not in God, the meaning of this parable is that forgiveness relieves you and the person you forgive from your bitterness, while condemning the other condemns you to it.

Love is the healer of violence. Faith is the opposite of fear. Compassion is the opposite of guilt; forgiveness is the opposite of bitterness.

Antidote 5

Be kind to your fellow citizens. Nobody needs your vindictiveness, but everybody needs your compassion.

Learn to deal with fallibility and imperfection, as you are fallible and imperfect.

Ask and listen, instead of judging and condemning. Be a superhero by helping and supporting your immediate neighbor.

Contradiction 6
Is God to Be Trusted or Feared?

The Calvinist interpretation of God gave little room for trust; the consequences linger on until today.

"Sin is indeed always in us and Godly people feel it, but it is covered." (Martin Luther)

The Protestant God has been defined as forgiving because He gives us hope and love, and unforgiving because He is expected to punish. However, implicitly or explicitly, He has historically been more of a punisher.

"In God We Trust" is printed in every dollar bill. It has become the motto of America.

Let us understand the words 'trust' and 'God' by searching in the handiest dictionary available. When we research these words in three different languages of Christian cultures, some differences take place.

Online definitions (Google, April 15, 2021)

ENGLISH

Trust, verb

Believe in the reliability, truth, ability, or strength of.

Example:

"I should never have trusted her"

SPANISH

Trust, *confiar*

Dejar una cosa al cuidado de alguien, especialmente en quien se tiene confianza. (Leave something to the care of someone, especially in whom you trust)

Example:

"le confiaron la dirección de la obra" (He was trusted with the project management of the contract)

FRENCH

Trust, *confier*

Remettre quelqu'un, quelque chose aux mains de quelqu'un, à sa garde (Put someone, something, in someone's hands, in their care)

Example:

Confier les clefs de son appartement au gardien.
(To trust the guardian of the building with the keys
of his apartment)

These are three definitions of the verb 'trust' in English,
Spanish and French. The verb has the same meaning;
however, each language (editor) chooses a different
example according to its culture and context, to best
illustrate the use of a word in a sentence.

Spanish and French give an example of the verb trust,
while English gives an example of the verb mistrust, or a
denial of trust.

"I should never have trusted her"

This example does not help understand the word 'trust',
is it because people may start trusting each other? In total
depravity nobody is to be trusted. The origin of total
depravity is the expulsion of Adam and Eve from paradise.
Eve invited Adam to sin. He should never have trusted her.

Online definitions continued (Google, April 15, 2021)

ENGLISH

God, noun

(In Christianity and other monotheistic religions)
the creator and ruler of the universe and source of
all moral authority; the Supreme Being.

Example:

"God, what did I do to deserve this?"

SPANISH

God, *Dios*

En las religiones monoteístas, ser sobrenatural único al que se rinde culto; es responsable de la creación del universo y del misterio de la existencia. (In monotheist religions, unique supernatural being responsible of the creation of universe and the mystery of existence.)

Example:

"Aunque sus características son distintas según las religiones, en el cristianismo, Dios es eterno, omnipotente, perfecto e infinitamente bueno y justo" (Although his characteristics are different according to different religions, in Christianity, God is eternal, omnipotent, perfect, and infinitely good and just.)

FRENCH

God, *Dieu*

Être éternel, unique, créateur et juge. (Eternal being, unique, creator and judge.)

Example:

Croire en Dieu. (To believe in God)

The Word 'God' has similar definitions in English, Spanish, and French. The French example that uses the word 'God' is neutral: the ability to believe in God. The Spanish example defines the characteristics of the New Testament God: infinitely good and just, eternal, omnipotent.

The English example:

"God, what did I do to deserve this?"

speaks of the rage of God (fate, consequences) acting upon the total depravity of an individual who is not able to understand how he sinned.

"In God We Trust" would then be an ambiguous and contradictory concept, where trust is defined by mistrust, and God is a punisher of total depravity.

> Christianity is by far the **largest religion** in the United States; more than three-quarters of **Americans** identify as Christians. A little more than half of us identify as Protestants, about 23 percent as Catholic and about 2 percent as Mormon. (Reid Wilson, Washington Post, Jun 4, 2014)

Protestantism

Unforgiveness and ethics cannot be understood without analyzing the religion brought to the British Colony: Calvinism. Luther and Calvin were the two reformers that based the Reformation on Apostolic traditions. John Calvin (1509–1564) was a French lawyer and doctor in theology. Damon Linker writes about Calvinism.

> Calvin and American Exceptionalism.
> Born five hundred years ago today, Calvin deepened the Protestant Reformation…formulating a sternly ascetic version of Christian piety that, as Max Weber powerfully argued more than a century ago,

inadvertently laid the psychological groundwork for the development of capitalism. Others have noted the surprising ways that Calvinist ideas helped to legitimize representative political institutions. Less widely acknowledged…is the profound impact of Calvinist assumptions on the formation of American patriotism—and in particular on the country's sense of itself as an exceptional nation empowered by providence to bring democracy, liberty, and Christian redemption to the world. It distinguishes American patriotism from expressions of communal feeling in any other modern nation—and that demonstrates our nation's…debt to John Calvin. America was New Englandized. According to historian John F. Berens, the motor behind this extraordinary transformation was the Great Awakening of the 1740s, which helped to spread theological concepts throughout the colonies… Woodrow Wilson's foreign policy outlook, including his proposal for a League of Nations that would make possible an era of global perpetual peace, grew out of his strong faith America's providential role in the world.

The World War II propaganda campaign frequently appealed to identical convictions. And politicians from both political parties regularly cast the Cold War as a quasi-eschatological conflict between forces of darkness and light—with God clearly standing on America's side of the battle. Even Adlai Stevenson…spoke in 1952 about the 'awesome mission' that 'God has set for us', which was nothing less than 'the leadership of the free world'. In more recent years, the cadences of the Calvinist consensus could be heard in Ronald Reagan's rhetorical evocations of America as a 'city on a hill' and George W. Bush's frequent assurances that history moves in a 'visible direction, set by liberty and the Author of liberty'. No commemoration of John Calvin's birth can be complete without recognizing this momentous American legacy. Whatever our views of American exceptionalism and its complicated human consequences, it is Calvin who deserves to be recognized as its unintended instigator. *(Damon Linker, https://newrepublic.com/article/50754/calvin-and-american-exceptionalism, July 8, 2009)*

Regardless of each individual's religious beliefs, there is a presence of God in the American culture.

"I pledge allegiance to the flag of the United States of America and to the Republic for which it stands, one Nation under God, indivisible, with liberty and justice for all."

This pledge, known by heart by many, is not only a patriotic statement, but the recognition of God.

We are immersed in a society founded historically on Protestant morale, whether or not you attend to Church, or whether or not you are a Roman Catholic or belong to any other religion of the world. You may or may not be aware of it. You may attend a Christian Church that never mentions Calvin. The first churches in the colony were Calvinist, better known as Puritan. Four centuries have gone by and churches with new denominations have been created.

While the God of the New Testament forgives, God from the Old Testament condemns. A more forgiving Catholicism was introduced to Latin America, while Calvinist Protestantism was introduced to North America.

> In the early years of what later became the United States, Christian religious groups played an influential role in each of the British colonies, and most attempted to enforce strict religious observance through both colony governments and local town rules…
>
> Laws mandated that everyone attend a house of worship and pay taxes that funded the salaries of ministers…
>
> Between 1680 and 1760 Anglicanism and Congregationalism, an offshoot of the English Puritan movement, established themselves as the main organized denominations in the majority of the colonies…
>
> The New England colonists—with the exception of Rhode Island—were predominantly Puritans, who…led strict religious lives. The clergy was highly educated and devoted to the study and teaching of both Scripture and the natural sciences… Government contained elements of theocracy, asserting that leaders and officials derived that authority from divine guidance and that civil authority ought to be used to enforce religious conformity. Their laws assumed that

citizens who strayed away from conventional religious customs were a threat to civil order and should be punished for their nonconformity. (Religion in Colonial America, Trends, Regulations, and beliefs, February 15, 2021)

Jacobus Arminius (Dutch, 1560–1609) was a Calvinist that grew unhappy with Calvinism. He wrote five points of disagreement as criticism describing how Calvinism was moving away from true Christianity (John Piper, Founder and teacher, disiringGod.org). After Arminius' death, his criticism derived in a movement called Arminianism and the conflict is referred today as Arminianism against Calvinism.

According to historian Professor Wrightinson, back in the 1600s, a majority of British Protestants started to differ from Calvinism, like Arminius did. The tension between Protestant Calvinists and Protestant Arminians grew to a point where Calvinists were no longer wanted in England. Some of them fled to the new continent to found their Church free of conflict, and others fled to Holland. (Deutch Revolt and Arminianism, Ryan M. Reeves audio conference, you tube August 2021).

Contradictorily, the five points written as criticism by Arminius became the five principles of Calvinism as we know it today. Arminius' criticism, as Dr. Ben Witherington III states, was aimed to Calvin misinterpretation of a God that chooses only a few individuals to receive His grace, as opposed to a God that offers His grace through unconditional love to all mankind.

The Roman Catholic God gives everybody the opportunity to be saved while the Calvinist God does not. (Arminianism with Dr. Ben Witherington III, The Remnant Radio, audio conference, you tube August 2021).

The following are the 5 Calvinist points (TULIP) now held not anymore as criticism, but as the true doctrine:

> "Total Depravity—Due to sin all of mankind is completely sinful, or 'depraved'. Every part of fallen man is corrupted by sin. He is a creature that is incapable of obeying the law of God. What is being taught is that our depravity is total in reference to our complete rebellion against God (Psalm 14:1–3) and our inability to do good (Romans 8:7–8) As a result of Adam's fall, the entire human race is affected; all humanity is dead in trespasses and sins. Man is unable to save himself."

If all men are to be blamed for their incapacity of doing well, it is only understandable that the individual will tend to be blameful against the fellow citizen.

> "Unconditional election, God's rescuing of sinners is entirely due to His own will and good pleasure. (Ephesians 1:5). Salvation is not brought about in any way by our actions or decisions. Remember, Scripture teaches that we are spiritually dead. Because of this we cannot and will not turn toward God on our own. Instead, it is God who elects believers to salvation."

Luther himself had a two-way opinion on this matter. On one hand, he believed that it is God who chooses some men to follow Him, leaving others behind. On the other hand, he also believed that some men make the choice to follow God and then God himself opens his arms to them. However, the common belief that got through in religion, education, and law, is the former, not the latter.

Let us make an analogy to our own lives. Imagine that you have six siblings and your father chooses only two to love him and be loved by him, how would you feel if you are not one of them? And how would you feel toward life, toward your siblings, toward God, and toward society?

This belief practiced by the first churches in America would make individuals feel rather neglected and would impact society for generations to come. It is also thought that capitalism was detonated by this belief because people would rely on wealth as a key to open the gates of heaven.

> "Limited atonement (1 Peter 3:18) Atonement refers to the forgiveness of our sins by means of Jesus' sinless life and sacrificial death. Christ atoned, or paid for, our sins on the cross. His sacrifice is completely 'sufficient' to save sinners, but it is made 'definite' only for those who God has chosen."

New Testament Catholicism believes that God died on the cross to save everybody who turns to God, while Protestantism believes that only the chosen by God are to be saved. Since no matter what good we do will not influence God to choose us for salvation, a son may not be entitled to the praising of his father, a child to the praising of his teacher, nor an employee to the praising of his boss. If the individual internalizes correctly these religious teachings, when the father, teacher, or boss praises a son or an employee, it shall be by his own will and good pleasure. Love and acceptance will not be gratuitous. Unacceptance is the default value, acceptance comes afterward only through God's grace. As we introject culturally and historically the Calvinist God, we may mistrust, reject, and be judgmental toward a fellow citizen without being conscious about it.

> "Irresistibility of grace. No one can be saved unless they are first drawn by God. (John 6:44) In short, this is the belief that all who are called by God to believe in Jesus will be saved. In John 6:37, God's sovereign election is not contingent on our response; those who are called by Him will ultimately obtain justification and glorification (Romans 8:28–30)."

When somebody seeks God, it is because God chose him in the first place. It is then that individuals will be saved. As the Calvinist God is introjected, there is no warranty that a Calvinist will be graceful to his neighbor. However, Dr. Reeves states that Luther's original point of view allowed also for individuals to seek God. It is when individuals turn to God, that the principle of Irresistibility of Grace is understood. (Ryan M. Reeves, PhD Cambridge. Later Lutheranism Part 2. You tube) The following is the fifth and last Calvinist point.

"Final perseverance of the saints. If you have been justified before God you cannot lose your salvation. Once a person is truly saved, this salvation is eternally secure." (reasonabletheology.org)

There is eventually comfort and eternal salvation for the chosen ones. All others will be condemned.

As American law is influenced by Calvinist morale, being a law-abiding citizen will not exempt the individual from punishment, since every citizen would be incapable of following rules and is absolutely corrupted. Therefore, every citizen believes that the other is corrupted, and that he himself is also corrupted in the eyes of the other. This is why being American may sometimes be a feast of victimizers and blame.

Back in primary school, Miss Alice, our American Morale Class teacher would lecture us once every two weeks in the school library in groups of 8. One day, she placed one coin near every chair before we seated. Back in the 70s, a coin could buy you lunch. She began talking about honesty and asked us to give our views about it. At the end of the class, she told everyone her experiment and shared the results: Maria left the coin on the floor, Tom and Luis took the coins and put them in their pockets, Carlos picked it up and left it on the table, and so on. I do not remember all. What I remember is that there were two kinds of kids in the group: the thieves and the good kids, the saints and the depraved. Every eleven-year-old tender morale was exposed in front of the group. The teacher was vindictive and did not respect the cocoon. She did not approach the 'thieves' after the class and counseled them. She did not apologize to us for having set us up in a controversial situation and exposed a human weakness. She tempted the group to sin, therefore acting as the devil? She was a smiling, righteous, silent bully with a plan: to bring up depravity. That is how we were raised and taught back in school: guilt infliction, bullying, shame. But not all was bad, the good kids, the smart and rule abiding, were praised and rewarded with a silver or gold paper star on the forehead, a monthly diploma, good grades, and recognition in front of the whole class (I am being somewhat ironical now). I was one of these praised students, and I kept the coin. There are no black and whites.

Protestantism and Wealth

As American political scientist Francis Fukuyama states, Max Weber theory has been debated.

"Weber's argument centered on ascetic Protestantism. He said that the Calvinist doctrine of predestination led believers to seek to demonstrate their elect status, which they did by engaging in commerce and worldly accumulation... (thus originating capitalism)

"The Weber thesis was controversial from the moment it was published. Various scholars stated that it was empirically wrong about the superior economic performance of Protestants over Catholics…

"It is safe to say that most contemporary economists do not take Weber's hypothesis, or any other culturalist theory of economic growth, seriously." (Fukuyama, Francis. "The Calvinist Manifesto" The New York Times, March 13, 2005)

However, vindictiveness and guilt, present in Protestant morale, are successful ways to obtain discipline in the work environment and therefore economic results in America, in other northern European protestant countries, and in some former British colonies. If not by Weber's belief that accumulation would secure a place in heaven for the rich, wealth and accumulation are a consequence of many and complex factors.

Protestantism and Law

As time passed by, law and religion merged, the fear of God was substituted by deterrence, and the rage of God gave place to law enforcement. Morale became ethics and Church became Law. American law mistrusts all individuals who are suspicious to the (subjective or objective) eye of the authority.

John C. Rao (born 1951) is an associate professor of history at St. John's University, director of the Roman Forum/Dietrich von Hildebrand Institute, and former president of Una Voce America.

Total depravity, says Dr. Rao, and the fact that human behavior in no way changes the destiny that God has determined for individuals demoralizes American culture as abortion or other debatable issues lose any sense in being debated. The Calvinist dream of a new civilization, the city upon the hill, excludes all other civilizations as they are worthless. The contradiction behind Calvinism is that if our behavior cannot change us, and we remain to be 'manure to the eyes of God', being moral or acting ethically has no reward. (Audio Conference on Calvinism & Americanism, Dr. John Rao, 2017 YouTube)

As animals and human beings, we are motivated by rewards, and the hope for receiving them. Having no reward, as John Rao states, turns our actions meaningless, which is another cause for anger on one hand, and on the other, it would explain the morality crisis of young Americans: drug abuse and debauchery, "…as abortion or other debatable issues lose any sense in being debated."

"Anyway the wind blows doesn't really matter to me. Momma, I killed a man…" (Queen, Bohemian Rhapsody, courtesy from 'the motherland')

In the law and order world, the concept of total depravity has become total trespassing; therefore the State mistrusts, controls, and punishes totally. However, a law and order driven society differs from a religious driven one.

The goals of both are the same, but the means are different. They both want a society where good is privileged over evil.

An important amount of marketing is aimed to tempt, and ultimately to corrupt the soul, at least symbolically. American capitalist society would then be fostering total depravity instead of fighting it. Capitalism, the baby of Protestantism, is depraved.

Patricia Roberts explains how Calvinist morality has permeated to law and law enforcement.

"A lot of American conservative Christianity is affected by Calvinism, not necessarily the most complicated aspects of John Calvin's beliefs, nor even all of what he said, but what might be called a popular (or lay) version of Calvinism…

"There are several ways in which lay Calvinism comes up, but here are the ones that are important for the question of what we should do (or not) about police violence:

"Humans are so corrupted by original sin as to be in constant danger of slipping into sin. Everyone knows what is and isn't sin (right and wrong are not only in a zero-sum relationship, but, at any given moment, what's right or wrong is absolutely clear). Sin is the consequence of giving in to sinful impulses (that we know to be sinful in the moment); that is, a lack of control. Therefore, only very controlling people can do the right thing, and only a culture of control can get people to behave well. The world is divided into saints and sinners, and that saints are the ones capable of self-control. The only way to get sinners to behave is to punish them; if you punish them enough, they will behave well; immorality and crime are (or should be) the same, because otherwise immoral people will not be punished and they will create a culture of immorality. Since immorality equals crime, this failure to control the sinners will mean that everyone—including the faithful—will be punished with a high crime rate. A nation that is not following God's obvious rules will be punished by losing its-dominance.

"If you accept all these premises, and I think they're a fair summary of what a lot of self-identified conservative Christians believe, then, it follows that we have to have a culture with a lot of punishment. Since immorality and crime are the same (people who are immoral will commit all the sins), then a culture that tolerates immorality will be a culture with a lot of crime…'People—all people—who are not threatened with punishment will sin'. Therefore, we have to have a police force that can punish people…

"If you accept all the premises of this version of Calvinism—people are basically bad, they only behave well if punished, right versus wrong is obvious to good people—then you can end up with thinking that the police should be able to punish people.

"Except for one problem. 'Police are people'.

"If all people are prone to sin unless threatened with punishment, then, if we give the police the power to punish people, some of them will use that power in a sinful way…" (Patricia Roberts-Miller, Retired Professor. December 14, 2020, patriciarobertsmiller.com)

Law is rational but the application of law may be irrational. A contradiction of society that follows from Patricia Roberts-Miller arguments is that if we all are sinners, nobody is entitled to punish the neighbor.

Pope Francisco states "all crimes are sins, but not all sins are crimes." To lie outside of a courthouse, for instance, is a sin, but not a crime. Americans should not punish each other for lying, since lying is a human condition that takes place practically every day, sometimes for a good cause, other times to avoid the rage of the neighbor.

Religion indoctrinates through persuasion and repentance to guide and correct the individual. Religion explains the difference between good and bad. Law, on the contrary, posts laws. Schools (and family) are expected to teach the young ones to follow them.

Legal consequences will take care of correcting the individual when he fails, and since all is restricted, he will fail. Adults are expected to investigate the law, find it and abide to it. Thus, the American believes that the other is also responsible to look for his needs and satisfy them.

> U.S. church membership was 73% in 1937 when Gallup first measured it. It stayed near 70% through 2000 before beginning to decline, to 61% in 2010 and 47% in 2020. (U.S. Church Membership Falls below Majority for First Time, Jeffrey M. Jones, Mar. 29, 2021)

Millennials are not attending Church as young adults used to in the past. If this tendency continues, millions of parents will not have learned morality from Church.

> "Hegel highlights the superiority of the civil State over the ecclesiastical State, marking the fact that in the civil State morality is not only safe but is

preserved in its true meaning, since it is not with blind obedience to precepts…on the contrary, in the free exercise of practical reason that chooses to act morally. The separation between law and morality is characteristic of the civil State and, consequently, it is what best adjusts to freedom, reason and morality." (Jorge Perez)

I differ from Hegel because the State, through schools and the Judiciary system, has failed to implement the infrastructure to teach the young ones. If morality is to be taught by schools, philosophy needs to be taught in High School, otherwise, where will teachers and students learn 'free exercise of practical reason that chooses to act morally' from? To learn morality from school rules or from posted laws is not to learn by reason.

Since truth, good, and evil are studied by philosophy, schools can take the social responsibility to teach morality through reason and discussion guided by teachers.

Frank Breslin, retired High-School Teacher, writes:

The Case for Philosophy in America's High Schools-Part 1

"Adolescents are a skeptical lot. Anything and everything is fair game to them…Criticism comes easily to these professional skeptics. Irreverence is natural (for them)… However, American high schools waste this irreverence by failing to harness and turn it to educational use. By not providing programs which could tap into this natural resource, they forgo their most valuable asset—the intellectual restlessness of youth itself.

"By barring this critical spirit from the classroom, high schools are saying that questioning is wrong and has no part in one's education. If one wants it, one must get it on one's own. This is the message schools often convey. This is regrettable, since what could be an opportunity to exploit and sharpen this critical temper is irresponsibly allowed to run into the sand…

"The study of philosophy is one such program which American high schools should introduce to channel this skepticism toward academic ends…

"Such a course would consider the various answers which have been advanced to these and similar questions over the centuries; seek to understand the historical era in which an answer arose; empathize with each answer to understand it better; analyze its respective arguments, and suggest objections and rebuttals."

(Frank Breslin,

www.heritage.org/crime-and-justice/commentary/reform-policing-what-makes-sense-and-what-doesnt)

From a philosophical standpoint, to establish moral values is not a triviality, it is the foundation of human relationships in society, peace, and civilization. Before laws were written, the ruling of the strongest prevailed. Individuals are all different; there is the faster and the slower, the stronger and the weaker, the more intelligent and the less intelligent. Law makes all individuals equal under the rule of law in order to bring justice to all.

To post laws and enforce them is not a pedagogic technic; individuals should reason human values and their hierarchy. Philosophy studies the evolution of human thought and the evolution of societies through history. Morality has to be reasoned in order to be truly efficient and truly humanized. Since philosophy is rarely taught in schools, American society is law abiding more because of enforcement than because of consciousness.

Sunday (Dominicus, Lord's day in Latin) is a time and Church is a place where morality is taught. Law provides none of these. Law provides no place or time to teach rules and comfort individuals, but it does provide a place and time for citations (punishment). Law does not teach; law enforces. Law provides no special weekday to abide rules nor gives a compensation for compelling with rules. It provides individuals with limited liberty and a non-incarceration condition, which may be kept in absence of crime.

As part of a church community, and depending on the community they attend to, individuals will be comforted by acting with faith, faith understood as the entire relationship with God.

Understanding religion is as diverse as there are individuals. Each person has his own understanding and relationship with God. Not having a relationship with God is a neglected relationship with God, with the creator, with the intangible, or with the ineffable reality of death. "For humans, to understand death is the motor of religion." (Ikram Antaki).

Hegel understands the religious individual in the ecclesiastic State as one that acts blindly and manipulated. Since it takes our whole life to understand God, I differ with young Hegel's interpretation because the religious individual can also understand God and act morally by love and conviction, not only by manipulation or blindness. To act morally, guided by love, is superior to act ethically, guided by conviction or fear. To the State, however, either one serves the purpose.

Sin, guilt, finger-pointing, fear of the rage of God and teaching good behavior and love compose the functional system created by the Protestant Church.

Crime, guilt, finger-pointing, law enforcement, deterrence, and the absence of fines or incarceration compose the functional system created by Law.

PROTESTANTISM	LAW	PHILOSOPHY
Bible	Written laws	Philosophy
Teaches	Posts laws	Enhances thought
Persuades	Controls	The individual reasons his own conclusions
Total depravity	Total trespassing	Humans are trespassers
Sin	Crime	Study of law and values
Guilt	Guilt	Does not make judgements, it questions
Fear of God	Deterrence through fear	Describes law and crime

Rage of God	Law enforcement	---
Moral values	Ethical values	Questions morality and ethics
Love	Respect	Consciousness
God	---	Beliefs are opposite to reason
Obedience	Compliance	Reason
Fulfillment	Liberty in absence of crime	Consciousness
Sunday	Every day	Philosophy enhances thought when needed
Mass	Posted laws	Philosophy
Congregation	Fellow citizens	Humanity
Church (the building)	Court	School, college, or on your own
Priest, represents God	Policeman, judge, enforce the Law	Philosophers
Moral counseling and advise	It is the individual's responsibility to know the law	A desire to understand the world

All this said, Americans are comfortable and content, or are used to live in this system. It is understood that this is the way things work, by compliance. Protestantism, republic, capitalism, democracy, and law and order, all intertwine and make the system functional in terms of having a booming economy and dominance over other countries.

Protestantism and Catholicism

American Catholic churches have fallen into indoctrination inherited from Protestantism. This is understandable because priests are American citizens living in society. Raised in a protestant country, it is only natural that they will bring their social behavior to Church. Andrew Greeley explains it.

Andrew M. Greeley is a Roman Catholic priest, best-selling novelist and a sociologist at the University Of Chicago National Opinion Research Center. UNDATED _ In a brief talk at the just-concluded Synod of Bishops on America in Rome, Chicago's Archbishop Francis George made a fascinating observation about American Roman Catholics.

> "The culture of America is essentially Calvinist and Catholics see their faith through the prism of Calvinism. Thus, American Catholics have a different vision of the church than do Latino immigrants, creating a sense of unease with American Catholicism for Latino Catholics… Certainly, the Puritan ethic persists in this country. The fixation on the miniscule elements of campaign fund raising, for example 'where was the president when he made certain telephone calls: in his private quarters or in the Oval Office?' could only happen in this country.

"On the other hand, the data available to me suggests American Catholics as a people are not Calvinist in their religious culture.

"…American Catholics are radically different from their Protestant neighbors and indeed becoming more so…

"George, like many other Catholic leaders, gravely underestimates just how Catholic is the religious culture of American Catholics, including non-Latinos.

"Communal loyalty among American Catholics is as strong as it is anywhere in the world and stronger than it is almost everywhere. Yet there is a problem that I will illustrate with a story:

"In a seminar at the University of Arizona, one of my students explained Mexican American religion. She talked at great length of the family feasts and festivals. Repeatedly, I pressed her for theological content.

"Just as repeatedly she continued in her description of festivals. Finally, when I said in near despair, "Lupe, what does it all mean?"; she replied, in some surprise, "Oh, I guess it means we believe God is a member of our family. When we have a family celebration, then God comes and celebrates with us." She paused and went on, "Of course, we should know the rules like you Irish do. That's why my husband and I have our children in a Catholic school, so they can learn all the Irish rules." She put her finger on the heart of the matter: American Catholicism as an institution of rules, laws, regulations and thus makes it a Calvinist institution – but only partly because of the Calvinist American cultural environment…

"Latinos will not find the institution of the church in this country nearly as appealing as the one in the old country. They will feel it is a cold, rigid, unsympathetic institution because the 'Calvinist problem' is not in the Catholic membership but in the formal institution and its leaders.

"I agree with the archbishop that we need a new, non-Calvinist model of Catholicism. It would be, I hope, a model that says while rules and laws are not totally unimportant, far more important is the truth that the God of Catholics is a God of family, festival, celebration, and implacably forgiving love."

(religionnews.com/1997/01/01/commentary-are-american-roman-catholics-really-calvinists/)

For Andrew M. Greeley, a non-Calvinist model of Catholicism would suit better American society and points out the need for forgiveness.

For New Testament God believers, or Roman Catholics, God is certain to forgive, though the individual may bring upon himself the consequences of his acts. God will recognize the morality of each individual and there is no limit in his lifetime when he can turn to God. The individual can turn to God in his youth or in his deathbed, truly repent, and God will open his arms. This comforting belief is the outstanding difference between Protestantism and Catholicism. The Protestant is guilty and uncomforted; the Catholic is forgiven and comforted.

The following are excerpts from talks (sermons) that I have heard in local Christian radio stations in San Diego, from February to July 2021. Some of the talks were in

English, some were in Spanish and they come from three different radio stations. The Spanish station is clearly Catholic. As for the English stations, I have been confused because they are a blend of Calvinist and Christian thinking, the latter becoming quite close to Catholic thinking; the message of unforgiveness and forgiveness, condemnation and salvation will change from one sermon to another. One priest may be speaking about predestination; 30 minutes later you will be listening to the power of the human soul to reach out to God. Confusing and opposite, so are American citizens, switching from unforgiveness to forgiveness out of the guilt felt after causing emotional damage. Vindictiveness can be as strong as a perfectionist locomotive, running over the other's feelings and fallibility. When the locomotive has run over too many souls, the individual slows down…or not, if lawyers are involved.

"You must obey God, you must obey God!" said one priest as he was ending his sermon about following the commandments. Law and order wants obeying citizens, not necessarily reasoning individuals. This is how this priest interpreted our relationship to the commandments. It is not incorrect but it is incomplete and vindictive.

I heard another sermon explaining the obedience to God. The priest said that obedience should be the result of trust and gratefulness toward God. It was an inspiring and rich message, full of examples and the tone was that of a loving God.

Another day, a woman called. She asked how long it takes for God's wrath to fall upon somebody. She had been hurt and wanted God to be an enforcer through the Old Testament's God's wrath. Living in a law enforcement environment, she was anxious to see God's rage happen. Perhaps she wanted to speed up the process by talking to an advocate of God over the radio. The priest explained that God does not act that way.

Tony Evans, a Christian pastor, gave a clarifying speech. He said that the Old Testament is about the wrath of God, while the New Testament is about the forgiveness of God. He centered his speech on the second one. He also said that the problems of the world are not about politics or economics, but people have to move to be spiritual and close to God. American founded Christian Churches in Mexico, from my point of view, are the blend of Catholicism and Calvinism.

In Relevant Radio.com, I heard the message 'restoration and reconciliation come from the heart'. Forgiveness is the message behind and society needs to turn toward it.

In another talk, speaking about humbleness, a priest said emphatically and repeatedly, "To be humble does not mean being weak or let others push you around."

This statement can be interpreted in different ways; however, if it were a religious justification for American dominance, in other words, fighting bullying back with dominance, this might not coincide with Jesus teachings. Jesus, however humble he was, does not show weakness of character in any of the four gospels, nor does he let himself to be pushed around, and he does so through wise replies. His crucifixion had a purpose. The pastor, God's advocate, would seem to be getting celestial justification for exerting dominance.

Dominance between fellow citizens is an enticement for conflict. Elliot Emory explains dominance rhetoric in Fourth of July addresses.

> "For over two-hundred years, in State of the Union addresses and Fourth of July orations, American Presidents have preached (that)…we must work together to restore our superiority among the world's nations. With God on our side, we shall continue the American Dream and fulfill our sacred Manifest Destiny (Elliott, Emory. 'The Legacy of Puritanism', July 28, 2021, nationalhumanitiescenter.org/tserve/ eighteen/ key-info/legacy.htm)"

Exerting dominance toward other countries may bring rewards for as long as it lasts, but dominance between fellow citizens can bring hostility and is a cause of anger.

The following point of view supports Calvinism.

> Reasonable.theology.org, "The Five Points of Calvinism, or Doctrines of Grace (TULIP) are merely summaries of what the Bible teaches about salvation. We do not revere these doctrines because they were taught by John Calvin, but because they are found in Scripture.
>
> These five points also serve as a helpful introduction to the beliefs of Reformed Theology. Although some of these doctrines can seem

difficult at first, I would encourage you to continue to look into these truths. As believers, our main concern should be conforming our theology to what the Scripture teaches. It is my conviction that Reformed Theology best captures the truth of God's Word in these and many other areas.
Calvinism has its footing not in the Reformation of the 1500s, but in the very pages of Scripture." *(https://reasonabletheology.org/five-points-calvinism-defining-doctrines-of-grace/)*

When in Luke 20:25 Jesus said, "give to God what belongs to God, and give to Caesar what belongs to Caesar" he marked the boundary between the State and God. State and God, government and religion belong to different worlds. When Calvin, lawyer and theologist, educated in both worlds, created a system that taught religion to society and enforced by means of law, he acted against Luke 20:25. The question posed to Jesus, "should man pay taxes to the Emperor because he follows God's teachings?" would in this case be, "should the State use God to enforce law?"

The rule of law, which is the enforcement of ethics, will not step back because the State has the monopoly of force. Religion has no monopoly of force, but has the monopoly of the relationship with God, so to speak. When these two separate worlds were mixed in the state-religious system called Puritanism, and in the mind of the citizens of New England, the State was favored, the relationship with God was not. What is to be enforced by law is the relationship between men. What is not to be enforced by law is the relationship between men through God nor the relationship between men and God. When the newly arrived Americans were enforced to go to a Church and to pay tithe, the Church was acting like the Roman Emperor. This condition has changed, but the cultural consequences linger on.

In an ideal world, in which Catholics believe, the individual would choose good over evil. In a depraved world, individuals will be led to introject law enforcement and fear of God's rage as one, contradicting Luke 20:25. Law is to be enforced by the State, God is to be preached among society. When State and God mix, citizens enforce their own will, thinking they enforce morale. This is why confused individuals punish their own neighbors every day.

Finland started a reform in school education back in the 1990's. A few generations of young adults have emerged after being educated in the new system. This system eradicated accountability in education. Children are not to be held accountable. The Fins, a country with a Lutheran Church, are also very strict in their social behavior. The new generations of Fins will certainly improve their society and the consequences of respecting the cocoon by not using vindictiveness as an educational resource are yet to be discovered in the upcoming years.

The idealism of Catholics and the fatalism of Calvinists contradict each other though inspired by the same God. American society, which is only 23% Catholic and more than half is Calvinist, holds within individuals the ambiguity of the irreconcilable contradiction between vindictiveness and forgiveness.

It is irrelevant to judge someone because he believes or not in God, for that is a private belief to be respected. What is important is to learn morality from available sources.

Morality does not come from movies, soap opera, school rules, sports club rules, traffic signs, posted laws, a neighbor, a best friend, law enforcement, or even teachers and parents who are only transmitters of the message.

There are three sources of morality:

1. Religion
2. Spiritual awareness
3. Philosophical reasoning

Through laws and good example, the state is a source of ethics, but not necessarily a source of morale.

It is up to Americans to determine what route they will follow as society in terms of teaching morality in the immediate future:

1. Ethics taught by the State's current resources: to post laws and enforce them (not pedagogic); school rules.
2. Morality taught by Churches (better if taught through forgiveness than taught through condemnation).
3. Morality taught by parents and teachers (their source of morality may not be clear in the next decades as people attend less to Church); good behavior mistakenly taught through guilt and punishment, rather than appraisal.
4. Ethics and morality discovered and rationalized by studying philosophy in high school and college education.

5. Guided spiritual consciousness finding true moral values in our soul.
6. Unguided individuals creating their own morale (subjective and with a risk of being depraved).

If nothing is done about it, the current society will intertwine with the stated contradictions.

The Underlying Morality Crisis

Americans continue to rate U.S. moral values negatively, on balance, and overwhelmingly agree that they are getting worse. These readings, from Gallup's May 1–12 Values poll, are the latest in the 18-year trend that shows similarly bleak findings.
A 47% plurality of Americans currently rate U.S. moral values as 'poor', 36% as 'only fair' and 17% as 'excellent' or 'good'. Since 2002, no more than 23% of Americans have held a positive view of moral values; the highest negative rating was 49% last year. (Megan Brennan, Research Consultant at Gallup, May 31, 2019)

Given that good and evil coexist, there is a need for law and law enforcement. However, this truth does not exclude the possibility of a society producing more 'good citizens and less law enforcement', as opposed to producing more 'bad citizens and more law enforcement'.
A society with high morale produces individuals with high morale. An unequal society produces individuals with

unequal morals. A diverse society produces diverse (cultural) approaches to morale. America is unequal, diverse, and with high ethical (not so moral) standards. It is also the country with more inmates in the world. This tells us two things:

1. There is an efficient law enforcement system.
2. Morality needs to be attended.

Ethics has failed because morality is lacking. American morale is as diverse as its immigrants; however, rules and laws tend to equalize ethics. Calvinism in all its denominations is the most spread morality.

> "The shift toward more liberal attitudes on a number of social and values issues has occurred across the age spectrum, not just among young people in controversial topics such as gay and lesbian relations, sex outside of marriage, having a baby out of wedlock and polygamy" A 25% increment has been registered across all of the age spectrum from 2001 to 2015. *(Frank Newport, Gallup Senior Scientist, 'Five Things We've Learned About Americans and Moral Values'. www.gallup.com)*

It would be debatable to classify these topics (gay and lesbian relations, sex outside of marriage, having a baby out of wedlock, and polygamy) as liberal or immoral. The Church will classify them as sins because they degrade family relationships and therefore society structure.

The question that rises then is, if American society is deeply Protestant, why does this 'immorality' occur? Let's recall Dr. Rao's point of view: "The fact that human behavior in no way changes the destiny that God has determined for individuals…" and the belief of total depravity acting both as cause and effect, "demoralizes American culture as abortion or other debatable issues lose any sense in being debated."

The morality crisis happening in America (and in a majority of countries around the world, each country due to its own particular reasons), would also happen due to a distancing from God, who is unheard, misinterpreted, or ignored. God understood not necessarily as Jesus Christ or God in Heaven, but God as a depositary of human spiritual knowledge and guidance for human relationships.

The strong cultural penetration of the American way of life through its current tools: lowly censored film, media and social media industries inspired in topics that degrade society, and greedy capitalism (profit oriented American companies), would be one of the many causes of a widespread morality crisis around the world.

Media industries would then need to be reoriented as to enhance better contents and produce better and superior thoughts in human beings. The government should recover its role as a Superior State that guides society toward a common good and not a facilitator of money-making enterprises.

The Self-Made Morale

The over stimulated individual in a rule and punishment system tends to set his own rules and punish the other according to his beliefs. Dominance, ruling, and punishment between fellow citizens are causes of anger. Dominance in a perfectionist society that is intolerant to human fallibility creates a hostile environment.

Is it ethical for a country to punish another country if, say, a commerce treaty is not followed? In this case, there are signed contracts where both parties agree to follow certain rules and sanctions. If one country does not follow the rules, a board of persons from the other country entitled by law to analyze the case will get together and evaluate the situation. These persons are not involved in the commercial transactions therefore there is no conflict of interests in their decisions. After debating, they will get to a conclusion and apply a sanction. The answer is yes, it is ethical because it was established in a contract, the facts were evaluated by a board of persons throughout a period of time and the sanctioned country agreed beforehand on the possible sanctions.

> A landlord is asked by the Home Owners Association to paint the exterior of the house. The landlord has a tenant living in his house and agrees with him that the house will be painted. Human fallibility is not late to appear and problems arise: the painter is absent for three days and the tenant gets angry. When the painter shows up, the tenant

punishes by not being helpful to the painter. The vindictive tenant will not give access to the balcony and will give contradictory instructions in order to release his anger. The painter complains. The painter finally takes one week longer than what was agreed between the landlord and the tenant to finish the job. The tenant threatens to punish the landlord by not paying one month of rent and finally concedes to pay one week less of rent.

Now, is it ethical for the tenant to punish the landlord? The answer is no, the tenant cannot punish him. The punishment was not mutually agreed beforehand, the tenant cannot be party and judge by definition and it is his sole interpretation empowering him, without the aid of other persons who are not involved acting as jurors. The painter was absent from work because his daughter had a legal problem (quite normal in a law enforcement society) and he had to help her; he had no choice. In the hierarchy of values, family is more important than work. There is a conflict of interests because the punishment the tenant wants to impose will favor him directly. Who is to say if the punishment should be of one week or one month's worth of rent, or even any punishment at all, the tenant?

We are constantly judging and making decisions throughout the day. How much tip should I give to the waiter? Did the painter paint the house as agreed? Should I pay him the total or should I punish and pay less? Who should I punish, the painter, the home owner, or both? Should the old pet live or die? A salesperson left me unattended and took care of somebody else, should I punish her by complaining to the manager? A driver made a right turn and did not turn on his blinker, should I punish him or not? My son is smoking marijuana but the state law allows it, should I stop him or not? Should I punish an employee? When should I ask for a raise?

When individuals no longer follow a solid moral source that cares for all aspects of life: family, couple relationships, the neighbor, work environment, society, nature, and God if that is the case, they will create their own moral values. The problem is that universal values may not be known nor ranked properly to the morally uneducated individual and his morale will be his own creation, changing according to circumstances and beneficial to himself. This kind of morale will most certainly lead to a depraved reality and in the context of American society the individual is likely to become a judge and enforcer. Depravity will then be a result of unguided self-made morality, with some reminiscences of religious morale and state laws learned from the past, shaped by the individual to favor himself. Depravity is thus a result of misunderstood, unguided morale and ethics, unquestioned by religion or philosophical thought, but disguised as 'own morality'. Total depravity would then seem to be the result of a total depravity frustrated combat. The *vindictive society* produces law abiding and law enforcer individuals who morally unguided are unwise. Each one rules an environment of his own.

Spirituality can guide us toward being morally aware, caring for the other and not caring for ourselves only. It can guide us toward doing the right thing and being fulfilled by it, not economically, but humanly.

Deepak Chopra shares this text about religion and spirituality.

"It's natural in troubled times for people to reflect on God and religion as a source of solace and hope, which matters more in a crisis. But with church services being so limited, not to mention the decline in organized religion that has continued for fifty years, God isn't the pillar of faith that past generations relied on.

I don't find myself thinking about spirituality in those terms, however. Like a winter coat that's put away in spring, for many people religion gets put away once the crisis has passed. Crises by their nature go up and down, but the deeper need for spirituality remains. This need is rooted deeper than solace and hope. It's the need for wisdom. Wisdom is a word that's open to skepticism and dismissal. Even people who think of themselves as spiritual are likely to think much more about issues like self-esteem and love.

Wisdom is much less personal but of crucial importance. It gives answers to why we exist and what our purpose is. Wisdom offers a vision of consciousness itself, bridging all ages and circumstances. It gets at the heart of reality. Ultimately the search for reality is what binds people who want to reach beyond organized religion and its perceived drawbacks." (Deepak Chopra, Spirituality means more than ever now, Yahoo life, February 16, 2021)

Antidote 6

Forgive yourself, forgive others.

Your neighbor is not totally depraved and you are not the rightful individual.

Let others compensate for their trespasses.

Do not punish your fellow citizens, you are not a judge, moreover, you are not God's arm.

Contradiction 7
Does the Spiritual
American Exist?

Spirituality is understated in the modern Capitalist world. Spirituality is a state of being where contradictions have no place.

The Spiritual Revolution is waiting its turn…

Yes, I constantly meet Americans who think and act spiritually, who enjoy being empathetic, who are generous and caring. Spirituality needs to be brought to consciousness and it needs to be enhanced.

What is being spiritual? What is spirituality?

It is not enough to eat organic and warm up in the solarium. There will be no social change without human change. And there are no human changes without changes of all. I hope that humanity finally understands that the great mutation will be that of the human soul. (Pierre Rabhi, Il ne suffit pas de manger bio pour changer le monde: conversations avec Pierre Rabhi, eBook)

As an American citizen, Deepak Chopra shares his thoughts of spirituality in the context of society.

"Personal desires and ambitions drive everyone from the ego level. Everyone has a self-image they need to protect, so the ego provides a very full agenda between getting what you want and avoiding what you don't want.
The private self is more ambiguous. Here you conduct an internal dialogue with yourself that can be very dark or very bright or everything in between. No one eavesdrops on the private self. You relate to it alone…
By contrast, the true self seems to promise nothing…Your sense of self brings you close to the origin of consciousness. It is the only valid starting point for journeying to the source itself. At the source, you discover something the mind cannot make: a flow of creative intelligence…'love, compassion, beauty, truth, empathy, wisdom creativity, devotion, the presence of the divine, and personal evolution'.

When the flow of creative intelligence enters your awareness, it enters through these values. They are not mind-made. They are innate in human awareness. No matter how primitive the ancient world might look to us in the modern world, having no electricity, smartphones, satellites, and television, every culture had the same sense of human potential as unlimited—such was the vision of all wisdom traditions. Yet no matter how exalted the achievements of the human mind, a single silent source was present.

All you need for a rewarding spiritual life is to meet yourself inside and allow your awareness to settle into its simplest state…"

(www.deepakchopra.com/articles/where-true-spirituality-begins/, June 10, 2021)

The Homo Politicus, The Homo Economicus, And the Homo Spiritualis

The new neo liberal world where globalized markets have become the new regime, has allowed for economic practices to conform a sort of a Global State where money and markets rule entire governments. The common citizen is unimportant.

Decades ago, the homo politicus cared about political and social issues that vinculated him to society. He would make sacrifices for the common good; he was an idealist constructing a better world. He believed in his social and political roles that would contribute to change the world and make it a better place to live. On the contrary, the homo economicus is the actor of the neoliberal world today. Every individual is considered an entrepreneur capable of creating value through developing his own skills, now called competences. The homo economicus is primarily competitive, competing against others to get a better position in an economy driven society. He will not sacrifice anything except on behalf of his own good. The nature of neoliberalism is to allow freedom interaction of markets, which are unequal by definition, thus bringing inequality to society in a new expression of oligarchy. Democracy, the government by the people that should bring equality to society is thus undone. (Wendy Brown, Undoing the Demos: Neoliberalism Stealth).

The narcissist postmodern individual has neither time to attend mass nor obtains any economic benefits from God. Spiritual concepts may divert him from making money; for him, philosophy has little value.

In contrast, the spiritual individual, who is not yet in the horizon as a declared social actor, is an escapist in the neoliberal world. Put aside by economics, the spiritual individual does not produce money by spiritual activity, but by playing a role in the capitalist world.

The spiritual individual has higher moral standards, does not belong to a church or does belong to one, active or inactively. He sees the other not as a resource to blame or use, but as an individual as valuable as himself through recognized differences. He practices self-control of thought through meditation, awareness, self-consciousness, or prayer. He preaches love silently with his deeds or outspokenly.

The spiritual individual knows how to live in the capitalist structure even though he may not agree totally with it. He cannot express his thoughts yet, unless surrounded by people he trusts. It would seem that it is not the time for the 'spiritual man' to arise; he is quite silent. He is inconspicuous in the working environment of the neoliberal world.

It is precisely because the spiritual man has no room in Capitalism, and because capitalist morality faces a critical moment, that it is time for him to earn its place.

The contradiction is that money will be top of the list for many; it is the driving force behind the homo economicus. It is the hardest thing to let go of. All efforts are aimed to its accumulation.

The spiritual man has another driving force that makes money no longer the sole priority, and that is *love*. However underrated love is in the neoliberal world, love is the strongest human driving force. It is the force that will make parents sacrifice for their children, as many other animal species do, which makes the argument only stronger and instinctive.

Love is the force that bonds children with parents and to the world. It is the force that will make someone to be with the love of his life and leave his parents love behind. It is the force of friendship; it is the force that bonds siblings. It is the force of creation, and when empowered by money, it can achieve incredible things.

On the contrary, narcissism, when empowered by money, is selfish and can be destructive for the individual and its area of influence. Surrounding himself with goods may not be, apparently or in the short term, destructive. In the long term, the narcissist, even though surrounded by people, lives in solitude.

Therefore the need of a spirituality vinculated to the economic system, a spirituality that will humanize social relationships and the working environment.

Roman law was written by a highly politest culture where gods and morale were intricate. Virtues were represented by Gods or Goddesses. Ancient Greeks believed that traditions were the way to teach good and evil to individuals. Socrates brought in the idea that it is through thought that the individual understands good and evil. In any case, law has a moral foundation. Morality needs to be brought closer to the capitalist individual.

Churches throughout history have not excelled in being spiritual or moral themselves; they have failed at times by being mundane and human. Nonetheless, they have been successful enough to transcend and teach morality to humankind.

Failures and clashes between religions and the homo economicus have relegated religiousness from the Capitalist society in the last decades. In America, religion is not taught in schools as a general basis, nor is part of the State. It is not legislated by law and order but is limited by it. It is not part of the economy; it does not produce money except for its own survival or wealth. It gets neither in the way of society nor economics. It is allowed to exist.

> Our founding fathers never meant to separate state and church, but instead just wanted to make sure that the government does not interfere with religion. Especially that it does not officially establish one particular religion or denomination over another or establish non-religion over religion. Separation of church and state' is a well-known phrase. However it is not found in the constitution of the United States. Here is what the First Amendment states in the Establishment Clause: "Congress shall make no law respecting an establishment of religion, or prohibiting the free exercise thereof…"
> *(https://www.partnerwith schools.org/separation-of-church-and-state.html)*

In many modern republics, the government ensures that religion does not interfere with the State.

Rationalism has pursued the religious thought and considered it fantastic and manipulative. This has proven to be true to a certain extent, but there are individuals that are both rational and believers, they understand the metaphors in religion as such and not as fantasies, and follow their God by reasonable thought.

It is irrational to try to explain the world through science and rationalism only, as it was to try to explain it through God only. The metaphors in religion are not to be taken literally, but to be interpreted wisely. However, their ambiguity gives room to all sorts of interpretations and science accepts only verifiable facts. On the other hand, science is limited to explain how phenomena occur and is unable to explain all, nor 'their ultimate origin'. The scientific mind can explain up to a certain point, and then runs out of explanations.

Lao Tzu's text, commented by Stephan Stenudd (Born 1954 in Sweden, he is a writer, astrologist, and aikido teacher) explains human values:

When everyone in the world sees beauty,
Then ugly exists.
When everyone sees good,
Then bad exists.
Therefore:
What is and what is not create each other.
Difficult and easy complement each other.
Tall and short shape each other.
High and low rest on each other.
Voice and tone blend with each other.
First and last follow each other.
So, the sage acts by doing nothing,
Teaches without speaking,
Attends all things without making claim on them,
Works for them without making them dependent,
Demands no honor for his deed.
Because he demands no honor,
He will never be dishonored.
(Lao Tzu, The Book of Tao)

"In the second chapter, Lao Tzu continues by presenting a consequence of what he stated in the first chapter." Explains Stephan Stennud. "Because the opposites of existence are united in a necessary whole, it's detrimental to separate them—either in deed or in value."

The unity of opposites makes up the world. We should not call one good and the other bad. There is no point in telling them apart at all, since they cannot exist divided. Nor do they make any sense when separated from one another…

Certainly, we appreciate some things more than others, but we must remember that we are able to do so only because we can compare them. The ugly is the mirror of the beautiful. So, who can say that beauty is only within the latter? That's why we are unable to find complete consensus about which is which. What one of us regards as beautiful, another will watch with indifference.

It's even so that each of us changes the way we see things, from moment to moment and from one perspective to the other.

Beauty is no object in itself, but merely the impression of one. It's in the eye of the beholder, and not a fixed quality of that which is beheld. So, we should treat our preferences with the appropriate modesty. And we should learn to appreciate the beauty in the ugly, as well as the ugly in the beautiful. None exists without the other, but within each other.

Good and Bad

We hasten to call some things good and others bad, but fail to recognize that such opposites are also deeply dependent on one another. Judging between them has little meaning. The prickled stem leads up to the flower of the rose. A forest is rejuvenated by fire, as is the soil by the merciless turn of the seasons. Night brings repose from day, and death gives room for new life. One is in need of the other.

Even when it comes to human deeds, judging them as good or bad is a risky business for the most experienced judge, as well as for a jury of twelve. There is rarely just one person responsible for a series of events, and within that person there is sure to be a number of contradictions. So, trying to decide on the character of a person in terms of good and bad is even less likely to succeed.

We are more complex than any book can cover. No person is simply good or bad. Both extremes are inside of us, and in a multitude of nuances. Any personality is a mystery beyond explanation. We can only observe the actions by which that personality expresses itself.

What we do is the result of a series of events and reasons. Few of them are at our control. Most of our actions are not ones of choice, but 'of necessity'…

"Not to mention the problem of what is good for one but bad for another. That's mostly the case. Therefore, modern philosophers prefer to discuss ethics in quantities: what is good for most people, or what is more good for one than it is bad for another, and so on. There is rarely an objective truth to be found, or a value that everyone can share…"

"Deeds of people may force us to react, but we are not helped much by defining those deeds morally, or even deciding on moral standards for all.

We make rules to bring a working order to society and to push society in the direction we want it to develop. We follow these rules when we can, and break them when we cannot constrain ourselves. The rules stipulate what the consequences of breaking them should be. That's all fair and square. There is no need to add a moral judgment to the legal one. For that, we simply do not have enough information.

If we allow morals to influence our judgments, we are unable to be objective. Then there is a risk that the punishment of a deed is far worse than the deed itself…"

Thus, the blamefulness of the individual is worse than the action to be blamed.

"So, the sage refrains from judging. He is very hesitant to interfere, or to insist that his opinion should be respected. He is reluctant to lead, and refuses to be followed. He is an example without pointing it out.

Since he never puts himself above others, they find no reason to rebuke him…

But the sage is not a person elevated above the rest of mankind. To Lao Tzu, anyone can be sage by simply following Tao. Those who do so excel mostly at being humble, not at all separating themselves from their fellow men. The sage is someone like you and me, but he or she has achieved true wisdom. *Sheng-jen* is a person with a refined spirit, who is modest about his place in the world and shows compassion toward others, whatever the level of their wisdom…"

"Lao Tzu has little respect for the ones who call themselves learned and clever. Instead, he stresses the superiority of simple reason, what we call common sense. To Lao Tzu, the sage is someone who excels at common sense…

Lao Tzu certainly had no problem with the possibility of women being truly wise. On the contrary, as will be seen frequently in the following chapters, he tended to regard the female qualities as far superior to the male ones.

He might have expected more women than men to be sage. Actually, what's to say that Lao Tzu wasn't a woman?" *(Stefan Stenudd. The Tao. www.taoistic.com/ taoteching-laotzu/ taoteching-02.htm, June 14, 2021)*

The spiritual man, or being sage according to Lao Tzu, is a state of mind reached by common sense, non-judgment, and understanding that good and evil cannot be separated and exist in each one of us. Human behavior is complex, contradictory, and most actions are not carried out by choice but by necessity.

There is no room for a common individual to punish another. It is the State, through teachers, policemen, and judges, who owns the monopoly of punishment.

The cause of economic discrepancies of the Capitalist world is the lack of order in thoughts and feelings. Society tries unsuccessfully to regulate the outside world, instead of teaching the mind to regulate itself. The law-and-order society punishes the act instead of educating the source of the act. The mind is mundane and practical. Intellectual intelligence fails; it can get a man to the moon, but incarcerates 2.3 million.

The Four Levels of the Human Being

Love God with all your heart, all your soul, all your strength, and your entire mind… (Luke 10:27)

We may agree that there are four levels of our being: body, mind, heart, and soul. No needed explanation for the first three, while the soul takes our whole life to find and understand.

To each ambit of our being we can make correspond an intelligence. The athlete develops his physical intelligence to master his movements. The student develops his intellectual intelligence by learning and reading. Psychology and Psychiatry help the mind to understand feelings and develop emotional intelligence. I define spiritual intelligence as follows;

The spiritual intelligence observes all three levels of the being separately and as a whole, of oneself and of others, within a system of values (morale) and spiritual laws. Spiritual intelligence acts on behalf of the common good.

Education in America is well centered on the intellectual abilities (your entire mind) and sports (all your strength). Emotional intelligence (all your heart) and spiritual intelligence (all your soul) are yet to be taught in schools.

Americans are aware of some feelings, and perhaps more aware of their own feelings and the feelings that are a threat from the other. There is a culture of interpreting verbal and nonverbal communication and implied communication. However, Americans are not taught to feel correctly, react, or interpret correctly. If they did, thousands of law suits would be avoided.

Any change that we plan for education will take two decades to begin to show, and generations to consolidate. Teaching these other two intelligences has been missed and is the healing to the toxicity of the homo economicus and humanity in general. The homo economicus needs to move two steps ahead and become emotionally and spiritually intelligent within the capitalist and democratic world.

Emotional intelligence teaches individuals how to feel and react correctly, away from the presence of learned past experiences that might produce biased or undesired neurotic behavior. Emotional intelligence, when taught in schools, will be of aid to the family and social behavior. New generations of families with better emotional skills will produce a better society.

Spiritual intelligence takes longer to explain and understand.

The observing self (Arthur J. Deikman) is the mind observing the mind, it is the mind being aware of the mind thinking and feeling. When the mind sees itself from outside, it is able to observe it as if it were another person, thus enabling a different awareness. We can all see the defects of other people but it is so hard to see our own.

The soul is a state of mind that finds peace and fulfillment; the soul guides the mind and the feelings. The soul can be perceived as another dimension of the mind, likewise the observing self. The observing self is easier to perceive. The spirit is harder to be aware of.

Spirituality means contacting with our own soul. As an American Indian from Washington once told me, "We all know the universal truths, but we do not remember them." When we contact with our soul, the moral values will appear as if we were learning them from religion. Since they were reasoned by our own mind and soul, later on they will be simply sensed. However, we need to keep in touch with our soul, otherwise, we will forget them.

In spite of how we may call it, soul, spirit, observing self, or consciousness it is there for us to develop.

They may all be ways to name and perceive the next level of consciousness, or being 'sage'. The difference between them might not be so obvious, nor is it necessary to differentiate them as long as we evolve our mind, our being.

Spiritual Awareness and Philosophical Thought

Deepak Chopra has held debates with scientist such as Michael Shermer, Heather Berlin, and Richard Dawkins. Confronted with the scientific method of investigation, Chopra's arguments may seem feeble because the fields of argumentation of spirituality and science have nothing in common. On the contrary, philosophy and science go hand by hand and are in the same fields of argumentation.

Philosophical thought and spiritual awareness lead to the realm of the intangible, the world of reasoned and sensed thoughts. Rational thoughts (philosophical reasoning) and spirituality are close in the sense that they both touch universal values in the next level of consciousness; they move us away from impulses and illogical reasoning, from senseless judgment and unemphatic behavior.

Philosophy analyzes truth. Spirituality uses moral awareness to sense and reason truth.

Consciousness is acquired through thought; we are not born with it. It is developed. Spirituality is also developed and sensed.

To the extent to which you can observe yourself and others from above (figuratively speaking) and understand them is the size, so to speak, of your sensed spirituality. All humans have the capability of being spiritual but some are yet to develop their awareness. Some people are not conscious of their feelings, so they go to therapy to learn about them. Others are not conscious of their spirit so they learn about it. Reading American authors such as Deepak Chopra or Donald Walsh are spiritual and religious approaches respectively. Practicing a religion, not a sect, and not being manipulated by it but deeply understanding it, is a religious approach; reading philosophy will be a philosophical approach.

Spirituality, religion, and philosophical thought are ways to be aware of our being and therefore understand the trivialities that may cage the body, the mind, and the heart in the daily life.

The spiritual cliché of people touching their own hearts, saying *namasté* or 'carrying a meditation matt' (Pretend It's a City, Fran Lebowitz and Martin Scorsese) is a revealed intention. To have spiritual intelligence is to understand that to be centered 15 hours a day on futile and unfulfilling actions and objects may not result in happiness or common good. Purchasing goods only brings temporary satisfaction. The way to solve every day's simple problems is not by calling 911 or a lawyer, or threatening, or exerting guilt. That will only drive us away from the solutions. How many lawsuits would be avoided by having two people talk over a problem, reaching out each one to their own spiritual intelligence?

Become a Spiritual Person

If you want to become a 'spiritual person', you will still be socially functional. You will develop a good emotional intelligence, you will be productive in the capitalist world, and you will develop enough spiritual intelligence to overcome mundane situations. You will live guided by spiritual laws, such as:

a) Detachment: let go of triviality, detach from objects that make you their slave, i.e. how much time do you spend on taking good care of your things as opposed to taking care of yourself or your loved ones? Let go of stubbornness and pride.

b) Acceptance: discern the situations that cannot be changed but only be accepted.

c) Fasting of the mind; control the monkey-like mind that jumps from one thought to another and often makes no sense. Like following a diet, the trained mind will not allow or 'consume' thoughts that are harmful, such as resentment, guilt, hatred, envy, but will focus on compassion, support, creativity, and productive work.

d) Non-judgement: understand the difference between good and bad, but stop being judgmental toward the other; rather be judgmental to yourself in the first place.

e) Unity, we are all one; what you do to others you do upon yourself, respect the other and respect nature.

f) Cause and effect: we attract what we most want, but we also attract what we most fear.

Trivial circumstances, such as who was supposed to do what, in what moment and in what specific way, only move our attention away from the real meaning of life. The energy deludes instead of focusing on working together toward creating and getting things done that are beneficial to all.

Let us be two souls caring for each other in the capitalist world, rather than two vindictive minds trying to make money from each other. Detachment and vindictiveness are opposites. We all make mistakes.

"It is what it is" is a spiritual phrase and a glimpse of how we could transform life as we understand it if we were to access to spirituality more often. This phrase entails the 'law of detachment' as explained by Chopra or 'nonaction' as explained by Lao Tzu. "It is what it is" means 'let go, you cannot change it no matter how hard you try'. Would you still want to go through all the effort to change it and fail?

The spiritual person lets go of or detaches from things, conflicts, stubborn ideas, pride, and insane ambition. Spiritual intelligence is based on acceptance of oneself and keeps a high self-esteem. It is based on acceptance of things too, and tries to deal with every day's problems, rather than trying to disappear or denying them. It is also based on acceptance of the other. It helps you have a real dialogue with the other, as you would like the other to have with you, rather than just using blame to relieve frustration.

Spiritual intelligence understands time and does not want the immediate satisfaction of robotized consumerism or selfish timing. Spiritual intelligence waits, respects, reasons, and enjoys the outcome. It fights frustration by trying to embrace problems and mishaps as there is only imperfection. It is the opposite of 'I waited too long; I want it now'.

The spiritual person avoids being judgmental to the other and does not need to forgive when offended, because there is no reason to feel offended. If offended, he knows it is a flaw of character and is quick to try to forgive. He who takes offense is looking for causes to take offense.

The spiritual individual is neither a spirit nor a soul, he has a social security number, works, and pays taxes. The spiritual individual interacts in society but does so wisely.

This is why spiritual intelligence along with emotional intelligence, need to be taught in society by all the means it has: school, law, family, and authentic religions.

Spiritual intelligence is unimportant to the capitalist world so far because it does not produce money. However, if the energy, time, and money used in lawsuits were used in creative activities rather than in getting even, the capitalist society would be benefited. Many lawsuits impoverish the clients but make the lawyers wealthy. Other law suits are about pride; self-esteem is the opposite of pride. Others are simply about making money; they are so lowly inspired that they do not even involve pride. And some law suits will be indispensable being there no other way to solve a conflict. Therefore, correct decisions will avoid wasting money in law suits.

From a spiritual point of view, money is pure energy. So spirituality is not the antipode of capitalism, it can become a greater source of it and its transformer to become a newer, fresher, more ethical capitalism. By a greater source, I do not mean producing more billionaires, who are an anomaly of a somewhat functional system. I mean a capitalism that is more fulfilling for more people. The anger that capitalism produces is that of consciousness of disparity. Leading a spiritual lifestyle in a capitalist world requires money and requires energy to achieve goals. Living a spiritual life does not mean that individuals will stop buying goods and live in a cottage. It means that individuals can learn to appreciate the goods they desire and will praise those who produce the goods. If the spiritual individual produces a good/service, greed and need will not be the main impulse, but a sane ambition and a desire to share and give. Profits are welcome of course, but not obtained abusing the other.

Governments would need to gain back control over capitalism and rule it, as opposed to losing it in neoliberal arrangements, and society in general would need to move away from the homo economicus and evolve to a homo spiritualis.

The Nature of Morality

"Morality is not just something that people learn, argues Yale psychologist Paul Bloom: It is something we are all born with. At birth, babies are endowed with compassion, with empathy, with the beginnings of a sense of fairness. It is from these beginnings…that adults develop their sense of right and wrong, their desire to do good and, at times, their capacity to do terrible things." (Gareth Cook, Scientific American. November 12, 2013)

A primitive sense of good and bad is innate, it is for society to shape and evolve it. Empathy and compassion are the foundation of morality.

What is chased is warded off. Morality is not to be chased, but taught. It is not to be taught by guilt, because guilt is a feeling that damages permanently self-esteem. Evil is not to be deterred through fear because fear is physical and leads to a flee or attack response.

Morality is physical, for it deals with correct or incorrect acts of the physical body. Morality is emotional because it deals with normal or abnormal emotional responses. Morality is mental because the mind understands or misunderstands moral values and is the cause of our physical acts.

When morality becomes spiritual and detaches from physicality (physical needs) and materiality (to lose or not to lose money, greed), morality becomes sensed, not thought, understood, not feared, wished, not conditioned.

Morality is to be taught spiritually, therefore the need of developing spiritual intelligence. However, children are not mature enough to understand the human soul. Children are to be convinced by the goodness of moral universal values. It is easily said but not achieved easily. Little monkeys are not easy to educate, and adults need to be educated first. Children are best taught by example. But once the child becomes a teenager, he is both tender and insightful enough to start his own way to consciousness.

Morality is to be taught through reasoned thought. Philosophy needs to be taught in high school and college, as it is taught in other countries.

We are all to connect spirituality, philosophical thought, and morality.

The Spiritual Man and Compassion

Empathy is the first step toward being spiritual, because one purpose of being spiritual is to transcend mundane and material attachments and care authentically for the other, as long as the other is acting in good faith. When an individual empathizes with the other, he becomes the other. When the other empathizes with us, and we empathize with him, conflicts will be solved.

In the industry, Design Thinking is a design process that involves 'empathy' (the understanding of the consumer's needs and experience by the designer) and testing, the latter being the verification that empathy was taken care of.

Society is moving in a certain way toward empathy for economic reasons; let it be essentially empathetic, not only for economic convenience.

> "According to Paul Bloom, a professor of psychology at Yale, most of us are completely wrong about empathy. The author of a new book titled Against Empathy, Bloom uses clinical studies and simple logic to argue that empathy, however well-intentioned, is a poor guide for moral reasoning…
>
> By empathy, I mean feeling the feelings of other people, says Bloom. So if you're in pain and I feel your pain I am feeling empathy toward you. If you're being anxious, I pick up your anxiety. If you're sad and I pick up your sadness, I'm being empathetic. And that's different from compassion. Compassion means I give your concern weight, I value it. I care about you, but I don't necessarily pick up your feelings." *(Sean Illing, Jam. 16, 2019, www.vox.com)*

Following Paul Bloom's precisions, compassion is a concept that better describes a source of morality, as compared to empathy. Merriam Webster defines compassion as 'feeling or showing concern for someone who is sick, hurt, poor, etc.'.

Ethics and compassion are related. There is no Ethics without the coexistence with the other. And there is not compassion without the other. Ethics produces rules and is enforced by law. Compassion produces care and should be brought in through love. Rules and laws are all about care and respect. A lawful society becomes vindictive, while a compassionate society becomes caring. However, while compassion (love) cannot be forced, law can be enforced. We cannot leave compassion alone to take care of society because it will be a failed society, and we cannot leave laws alone to take care of society because law enforcement produces fear. The need to humanize the lawful republic is evident. Ethics and compassion go hand by hand.

If God and religion are rapidly being segregated from society, or contradictorily, they are being taught in an unforgiving way, can the State be forgiving? Many trespasses are forgiven or treated as misdemeanors. Others are restituted by small community work. Let us have more of that.

If enforcement and incarceration are less needed, a better moral judgement from individuals will be the cause.

Is America a Fertile
Soil for the Spiritual Man?

America would seem, from all countries in the world, the least fertile soil to enhance a transformation from the *homo economicus* to the *homo spiritualis*. It is the Capitalist country by excellence. Dominance is not compassionate.

On the other hand, America has a strong sense of community that constantly achieves new goals by massive team work and nationalism. When Americans perceive a common good, they will move toward it as a unity. From this standpoint, America is one of the most fertile countries in the world to house any transformation, as long as a true benefit is perceived. The movie 'Pay it Forward' (Mimi Leder, 2000) although fiction, shows an inspiring spiritual communitarian behavior.

> A teacher (Kevin Spacey) assigns homework to his students: to come up with a plan that will change the world by direct action. Twelve-year-old Trevor comes up with the idea of creating a chain of good actions. He who receives a good action shall pay it forward to three people. His plan is impressive. He starts by favoring a homeless man inviting him to spend a night in his home. The chain begins and soon hundreds of people are paying forward the good action they have received. A reporter is intrigued when he loses his car and a stranger approaches to give him the keys of his own Jaguar. While this happens, Trevor is a bullied child in his school. One day after classes, he defends a friend that is also being bullied but in doing so is unfortunately deadly stabbed with a knife. Meanwhile, the pay it forward chain he created has gone nationwide. Hundreds of people gather out of his house with candle lights to pay respects for his death.

The American will become the new spiritual man if this transformation is linked correctly to Capitalism, global leadership (not global dominance only), and to a truer, guided freedom of the individual. If money is understood as energy, individuals can learn to develop a better relationship with it. Energy is not stagnant. Accumulated wealth is stagnant, energy transforms lives.

Ethics are present in government policies. Policies are written to favor Americans for the betterment of their lives. When policies are publicly discussed, they are backed by ethical judgements. When the State is confronted to the massive shootings dilemma, it is evident that spiritual intelligence is needed to transform related policies and laws.

> Let us have the ethics of the sage, not the ethics of the saint nor the ethics of the hero. (Michel Onfray, A Hedonist Manifesto: The Power to Exist).

I have mentioned the overwhelming consciousness of the other in the American society in terms of not trespassing. The American has learned to abide to law through guilt and fear, which brings him to care for the other in a certain way. Caring for the other authentically instead of fearing or avoiding the other is needed. No change can happen if it is not idealist by principle. To be practical is a paralysis because the status quo is honored.

Spiritual intelligence is about connecting with our own soul, and bringing individuals to care for the other as a human being. Capitalism has dehumanized relationships, because the bottom line of everything is prized in dollars. It is through spiritual intelligence that this can be reversed. The *homo spiritualis* as opposed to the *homo economicus* may use his body, mind, and heart to obtain money as a means to enjoy life. Life is to be enjoyed with the abundance needed 'with the other', not 'without the other'.

Americans are motivated, ambitious, and strong. They are achievers and enjoy success. The fear to trespass the other, and the anger for being trespassed, can turn into the pleasure of coinciding and sharing. The need to exert guilt can become the pleasure of sincere praising, if only we stop and think about the accuracies and precisions of the other. Legal actions can be avoided if individuals agree to have a conversation. Law enforcement can give room to exhortation, in many cases. Arms should be banned, and shooters can in turn cry for attention. A threat can become a plead for compassion.

Americans shall recover their ability to talk to each other. Blaming or threatening is not talking. Talking and not letting the other talk is a monologue. Hanging the phone is the opposite of talking. Communicating a long list of reproaches is not opening up a conversation. Not listening and not empathizing is not talking.

Behaving like a bully is not talking. Punishing the other is being coercive. Calling your lawyer is not talking. Vindictiveness destroys all, don't be the Lone Ranger shooting 360 degrees to kill imperfection and otherness. Don't be the resentful son of society. Talk, get together, negotiate, empathize, listen.

I am a firm believer that the American holds within the power to transform the essence of the homo economicus into the homo spiritualis the world deserves. The global cultural penetration of America can influence other countries as well, making this a better world.

Education is always the key.

America shall gleam,
not from silver and gold,
not from steel dipped in blood
but from leading with love.
America shall command,
not with bankers and tanks,
not with greed and attacks,
but caring for all.

Conclusion

Guilt and vindictiveness have a traceable origin that goes back to early Protestantism (Puritanism). As generations passed by, they were introjected by people and became part of the American culture, as well as of the culture of other protestant countries around the world. Capitalism has only detonated and reinforced them. Because their origin is religious, the solution to move away from guilt and vindictiveness needs to be through a different religious approach, that of forgiveness. As many individuals have suffered from bullying, guilt, legal actions, collection, and so on, spiritual action is needed in order to heal and stop the chain reaction of a society that only reproduces itself without evolving. Hurt people hurt people. Religion, philosophical thought, and spiritual wisdom will make individuals evolve to a homo spiritualis.

Assertiveness and Appeasement

Erik Schwarz researches and rephrases a lexicon that is helpful to communicate his DAS theory: Dominance, Aversion, and Submission, which is an analysis of power and dominance in society (DAS2-theory: the awareness of power. Pp 19–32 2017).

Aggression (DAS): The fighting instinct in beast and man which is directed against members of the same species.

Appeasement (DAS): Embodied co-evolved intraspecies reactions that are directed toward stopping a dominant individual of the species from causing more or severe (bodily) damage.

Assertiveness (DAS): The proactive attitude to resolve one's needs, by means different than violence.

Authority (vernacular): The power to command, determine, demand obedience, enforce rules, and judge.

Aversion (DAS): Renouncing to attain control over a situation, neither directly or as an aide.

Conflict (DAS): the incompatibility of wills.

Control (DAS): The capacity to intentionally influence events and others, with the goal of attaining certainty of the outcomes.

Dominance (Heinrich & Gill-White) The social asymmetries that result from agonism—that is, force or force threat (e.g. Aggression, intimidation, violence).

Frustration (DAS): The discomfort produced by the suppression of a consummatory act, or the necessity to return to homeostasis.

Hostility (DAS): a) The will to cause frustration, b) contemptuous opposition (toward a party in conflict with).

Humiliation (DAS): The loss of status, possibly with a fall in rank.

Influence (DAS): The condition where acts and opinions of one person (entity) become an input for the decision-making of another.

Leadership (DAS): The use of influence to summon the efforts of others to advance a cause and control those against it.

Righteous indignation (DAS): the deep-seated emotion realized when we perceive someone mistreated past any legitimate limit, attempting his (human) rights or even dignity.

Submission (DAS): Yielding one's will to some external being, allowing it to exercise control.

Presumptuous *dominance* makes the psychological environment a violent one, and social relationships prone to conflicts.

When a *conflict* appears, *assertiveness* shall be used to influence the other party. If the other party were to use *aggression*, *appeasement* would be the wisest resource.

If witness of an *aggression* (in a conflict), *righteous indignation* will be of use in order to ask for or provide help.

If, as a result of the *conflict*, you are right and the other party is partially or even totally wrong, *leadership* will help you negotiate a solution.

Submission is recommended when you are dealing with an *authority*. However, if you are not an *authority*, do not behave like one and do not expect *submission*; otherwise you will only be pretentious. Remember that for you to become an authority, a higher entity shall endorse you.

Rather than using *hostility* or *humiliation*, which will provoke *frustration*, be *assertive*.

Antidotes' Summary and Application

Many Americans have forgotten the basic ways to relate to each other. They have evolved so much as a society in creating abundant laws that they have involved. The exaggeration of ethics has become unethical.

Citizens need to take one step back, or go to the next level of consciousness, where pride is set aside and solutions are the focus.

The antidotes I mentioned in all chapters can be translated into actions; they are only a glimpse to what the American society can do while greater measures are taken to restructure the system.

CUSTOMER SERVICE

When people are ready to call the manager:
Can I tell you what I want from you?
When people are ready to dispute a balance:
Can we find together a solution for you to repair/replace so that I can pay you? I can also see the effort and good work in supplying the product/service.

COLLECTION

When an individual, an institution, or a government office is ready to enforce/sue/penalize for lack of payment:
Your payment is overdue, when can we expect payment? Can you share the hardships that you are going

through? These are the options to request a payment plan or to obtain a late fee condonation.

FAMILY

When a parent punishes and exerts guilt:

You know I love you. I don't like what you did, it made me feel bad, can you tell me why you did it?

You know I love you and I get angry because I am worried about you. Can you please…

When a spouse /couple is planning to flee:

You know I love you. We have come a long way together, can we talk?

You know I love you. Can I tell you what I do not like?

LEGAL

When individuals are ready to sue:

-I know we are angry at each other, but…can we meet and talk? I'll treat you a coffee.

When individuals have already sued:

Listen, I got carried away, I apologize for getting my lawyer involved, I still believe we can come to our senses…

I know you called your lawyer. There is no need for this, can we talk?

MONEY

When your judgment is blurred by greed or need, and you want to take advantage of your spouse, sibling, friend, parent, or neighbor: stop.

PAYMENT

When you owe money to someone and you have the money:

I owe you money and time is passing by without us coming to a solution. Let us find it soon so I can pay you.

When you owe money to someone but you do not have it:

Things changed abruptly and I am momentarily out of money. Please be patient and I will pay you.

PUNISHMENT

When you want to punish someone that you are not entitled to punish (you are only entitled to punish your own children or your students if you teach children and teenagers):

You have not complied with what you were supposed to comply. Can we figure out a solution together?

SCHOOL

When a teacher assumes disobedience and is about to punish:

Can you tell me why you did this? Can you tell me what happened?

WORK

When you are about to terminate an employee without absolute certainty of your judgement:

I have been told that/I perceive that…how can you convince me that it is not true?

When as an employee you are ready to quit but are not absolutely certain about it:

I am not achieving what I expect in terms of recognition/money/fulfillment/contribution… can we both think how to make it work?

Bibliography

Brown, W. *Undoing the Demos: Neoliberalism Stealth.*

Chopra, D. *7 Spiritual Laws of Success.*

Chul Han, B. *The Palliative Society: Pain Today.*

Chul Han, B. *The Transparency Society.*

Grisham, J. *The Rooster Bar.*

Dussel, E. (1990) *Ethics of Liberation.*

Holy Bible.

Marinoff, L. *Plato not Prozac.*

Perez, S. (2007) *Hegel: his concept of freedom*, Mexico: Casa Juan Pablos Universidad Autonoma Metroplitana, 103–117.

Rousseau, J. *The Social Contract.*

Sandel, M. J. (2021) *The Tyranny of Merit: What's Become of the Common Good?*

Schwarz, E. (2017) *DAS2 Theory: The Awareness of Power*, Mexico, 19–32.

Tzi, L. *The Book of Tao.*

Weber, M. *The Protestant Ethic and the Spirit of Capitalism.*

Blogs

Terrel, M. 'The Observing Self', *unk.com/blog.*

Journals

Cook, G. (2013) 'The Moral Life of Babies', *Scientific American.*

Fukuyama, F. (2005) 'The Calvinist Manifesto', The New York Times.

Feinman, J. M. (2020), The Washington Post.

Hitchens, C. (2004) 'Unfairenheit 9/11', *Slate*, Web. 20 May.

Illing, S. (2019) *Jam*, www.vox.com.

Lehrer, E. (2019) www.thehill.com.

Organizations

Brennan, M. (2019) *Research Consultant at Gallup*, https://news.gallup.com/poll/257954 2019.

Chopra, D. 'Spirituality means more than ever now', yahoo.life, February 16.

Edward, J. (2021) 'Capitalism Has Not "Lifted Billions Out of Poverty" Nor Has Economic Growth "Benefited The Environment"', *The Specter of Communism*.

Elliott, E. (2021) 'The Legacy of Puritanism', national humanities
center.org/ tserve/eighteen/ekeyinfo/legacy.htm.

Fangmann, A. (2015) 'Illinois Supreme Court Strikes Down Pension Cuts', *World Socialist Web Site*, Web. 20 May 2015.

Newport, F. 'Five Things We've Learned About Americans and Moral Values', *Gallup Senior Scientist*,
www.gallup.com.

Breslin, F. (2016) Contributor, Retired High-School Teacher, Sep. 03, 2016 The Case for Philosophy in America's High Schools—Part 1

www.heritage.org/crime-and-justice/commentary/reform-policing-what-makes-sense-and-what-doesnt), McAfee, J. (2013) whoismacafee.com, Patricia R. (2020) Retired

Professor, Writing Center Director, Scholar of train wrecks in public deliberation.

U.S. Church Membership Falls below Majority for First Time (Jeffrey M. Jones, Mar. 29, 2021 *www.partnerwithschools.org*/separation-of-church-and-state.html reasonabletheology.org
"Calvinism & Americanism" Dr. John Rao, 2017 You Tube reasonabletheology.org/five-points-calvinism-defining-doctrines-of-grace/
religionnews.com/1997/01/01/commentary-are-american-roman-catholics-really-calvinists/religionnews.com/1997/01/01/commentary-are-american-roman-catholics-really-calvinists/

Stenudd, S. (2021) The Tao. *www.taoistic.com*/ taoteching-laotzu/taoteching-02.htm.

worldpopulationreview.com/country-rankings/freest-countries.

www.academia.edu/35495485/
The Most Litigious Countries in the World, July 10, 2021.

www.goodtherapy.org/learn-about-therapy/issues/guilt

www.deepakchopra.com/articles/where-true-spirituality-begins/, June 10, 2021

www.ushistory.org/us/3c.asp

You Tube

Antaki, I. (2000) 'Toward a Citizen Ethics', You Tube.

Johnson, R. (2018) 'A New Foreign Policy: Beyond American Exceptionalism', Interview with Jeffrey Sachs, Columbia University Press.

Reeves, R. M. (2021) 'Deutch Revolt and Arminianism', You Tube.

The Remnant Radio. 'Arminianism with Dr. Ben Witherington III', You Tube August 2021.

Rao, J. Dr. (2017) 'Calvinism & Americanism', YouTube.

Reeves, R. (PhD Cambridge) 'Later Lutheranism Part 2'. Piper, J. disiringGod.org.

Reich, R. (2021) 'What if We Actually Tax the Rich?', YouTube.